Unlocking Coding: Mastering 40+ Programming Languages

By

M J Kenneth

Table of contents

What is computer programming

Computer programming, often referred to simply as programming, is the process of designing, writing, and maintaining sets of instructions or code that a computer can execute to perform specific tasks or achieve particular goals. These instructions are written in programming languages, which are formalized and structured methods of communicating with computers.

Here are some key aspects of computer programming:

> Writing Code: Programmers write lines of code using a programming language. This code can range from simple instructions to complex algorithms.
>
> Problem Solving: Programming often involves problem-solving. Programmers need to break down tasks or problems into smaller,

manageable steps that a computer can understand and execute.

Programming Languages: There are numerous programming languages available, each with its own syntax and features. Some popular programming languages include Python, Java, C++, JavaScript, and Ruby, among others. The choice of language depends on the project's requirements and goals.

Debugging: Programmers must test their code to identify and fix errors, which is known as debugging. Debugging is an essential part of the programming process.

Optimization: After code is functional, programmers may optimize it to improve its efficiency and performance. This can involve making code run faster or use fewer system resources.

Software Development: Programming is a fundamental aspect of software development. Programmers work on

various types of software, including desktop applications, mobile apps, web applications, games, and more.
Hardware Interaction: Programmers can write code to interact with hardware components, such as sensors, cameras, and microcontrollers, enabling the automation of various tasks.
Algorithms and Data Structures: Programmers often work with algorithms and data structures to solve specific problems efficiently. These are fundamental concepts in computer science.
Continuous Learning: The field of computer programming is constantly evolving. Programmers must continuously update their skills and stay current with new technologies and programming languages.
Collaboration: Many software projects involve teams of programmers who collaborate to develop and maintain

software applications. Effective communication and teamwork are essential in such scenarios.
Computer programming is a versatile skill used in various industries, including software development, data science, artificial intelligence, web development, and more. It plays a crucial role in shaping the digital world by creating the software and applications that power our devices and systems.

Types of computer programming languages

There are many programming languages available, each designed for specific purposes and with unique features. The choice of a programming language depends on the project's requirements, the intended platform, and personal preferences. Here are some of the most common types of programming languages:

High-Level Programming Languages:

These languages are designed to be more human-readable and easier to understand, making them suitable for a wide range of applications.

- Python: Known for its simplicity and readability, Python is popular in web development, data analysis, artificial intelligence, and scientific computing.
- Java: A versatile language used for building Android apps, enterprise-level applications, and web services.
- C#: Developed by Microsoft, C# is commonly used for developing Windows applications, games (with Unity), and web services (with ASP.NET).
- Ruby: Known for its elegant syntax, Ruby is often used for web development, particularly

with the Ruby on Rails
framework.

- Swift: Developed by Apple, Swift
  is used for iOS and macOS app
  development.

-

Low-Level Programming Languages:

These languages are closer to machine
code and provide more direct control
over hardware.

- C: A widely-used language for
  system programming, embedded
  systems, and low-level tasks.
- C++: An extension of C, C++ is
  used for game development,
  system software, and
  performance-critical
  applications.
- Assembly Language: The
  lowest-level programming
  language that uses
  human-readable mnemonics to

represent machine code instructions.

Scripting Languages:

These languages are often used for automating tasks and are interpreted rather than compiled.

- JavaScript: Primarily used for web development to create interactive web applications.
- PHP: Used for server-side scripting to develop dynamic websites and web applications.
- Perl: Known for its text processing capabilities and used in system administration, web development, and more.

Functional Programming Languages:

These languages treat computation as the evaluation of mathematical functions and are known for immutability and declarative programming.

- Haskell: A purely functional language used in academia and some niche areas of industry.
- Scala: Combines object-oriented and functional programming and is often used for large-scale systems.
- Elixir: Known for its concurrency support and used for building highly scalable and fault-tolerant systems.

-

Domain-Specific Languages (DSLs):

These are designed for specific tasks or industries, such as SQL for database querying or HTML/CSS for web page markup and styling. Markup Languages: While not programming languages in the traditional sense, markup languages like HTML (for structuring web content) and XML (for data interchange) play essential roles in web development and data processing.

Data Science and Statistical Languages:

Specialized languages for data analysis and manipulation.

- R: Designed for statistics and data analysis, often used in academia and data science.
- Julia: Known for its high-performance computing capabilities and used for scientific and numerical computing.

Scripting and Automation Languages:

Used for task automation and scripting.

- Bash (Shell Scripting): Used for automating tasks in Unix-like operating systems.

- PowerShell: Used for scripting and automation in Windows environments.

These categories are not mutually exclusive, and many programming languages can be used for various purposes. The choice of a language depends on the specific needs and goals of the project.

Importance of programming languages
High-level programming languages are designed to provide a more human-readable and abstracted way of writing code compared to low-level languages. They offer a range of functions and features that make it easier for programmers to develop software, solve complex problems, and increase productivity. Here are various functions and features of high-level programming languages:

Abstraction: High-level languages provide a higher level of abstraction from the underlying hardware and system details. This allows programmers to focus on solving problems without needing to worry about the intricate details of the computer's architecture.

Readability: High-level languages are often designed to be easily readable by humans. They use human-readable keywords, syntax, and structures, which makes it easier for programmers to understand and maintain code.

Portability: Code written in high-level languages is often portable, meaning it can be run on different platforms and operating systems with minimal modifications. This reduces the need for extensive platform-specific coding.

Productivity: High-level languages are known for their ability to boost programmer productivity. They typically offer built-in functions, libraries, and frameworks that simplify common tasks, allowing programmers to develop software more quickly.

Scalability: High-level languages can be used for both small-scale and large-scale projects. They provide tools and abstractions that help manage the complexity of larger applications, making it easier to scale and maintain codebases.

Support for Object-Oriented Programming (OOP): Many high-level languages support OOP principles, enabling the creation of classes, objects, and encapsulated code structures. This promotes code modularity and reusability.

Memory Management: High-level languages often handle memory management automatically or provide garbage collection mechanisms, reducing the risk of memory-related bugs like memory leaks.

Standard Libraries: High-level languages come with extensive standard libraries that offer pre-written functions and modules for common tasks such as file I/O, data manipulation, network communication, and more. These libraries save time and effort for programmers.

Community and Ecosystem: High-level languages usually have active communities and ecosystems. This means programmers can access a wealth of resources, third-party libraries, and online forums for support and collaboration.

Rapid Prototyping: High-level languages are well-suited for rapid prototyping and iterative development. Programmers can quickly implement and test ideas, making it easier to refine and improve software.

Cross-Disciplinary Use: High-level languages are versatile and can be used across a wide range of domains, from web development to data science, scientific computing, artificial intelligence, and more. This versatility makes high-level languages valuable for programmers in various fields.

Examples of high-level programming languages and their specific functions:

- Python: Known for its simplicity and readability, Python is used extensively in web development, data analysis, scientific computing, machine learning, and automation.
- Java: Renowned for its platform independence, Java is widely used in enterprise software development, Android app development, and web services.
- C#: Developed by Microsoft, C# is used for building Windows applications, games (with Unity), and web services (with ASP.NET).
- Ruby: Often associated with web development, Ruby is used with the

Ruby on Rails framework to create web applications.

- Swift: Specifically designed for iOS and macOS app development, Swift is known for its performance and safety features.

In conclusion, high-level programming languages provide programmers with powerful tools and abstractions to develop software efficiently, improve readability, and enhance productivity. They are essential in modern software development and offer a wide range of functions to meet diverse programming needs.

How to program with python

Programming with Python involves a series of steps that include writing, testing, and running Python code to achieve specific tasks or solve problems. Here's a step-by-step guide on how to get started with programming in Python:

Install Python:

- First, ensure that Python is installed on your computer. You can check if Python is already installed by opening a command prompt (or terminal on macOS and Linux) and typing python --version or python3 --version. If Python is not installed, download the latest version from the official Python website (https://www.python.org/downloads/) and follow the installation instructions for your operating system.

Choose a Code Editor or IDE (Integrated Development Environment):

- You can write Python code in a basic text editor, but using a code editor or IDE designed for Python development is highly recommended. Some popular options include:

- Visual Studio Code (VSCode)
- PyCharm
- Jupyter Notebook (great for data science)
- IDLE (Python's built-in IDE)
- Sublime Text

Write Your First Python Program:

- Open your chosen code editor or IDE.
- Create a new Python file with a .py extension (e.g., hello.py).
- Write your Python code. Here's a simple "Hello, World!" example:

```python
print("Hello, World!")
```

Run Your Python Program:

- Save your Python file.
- In your code editor or IDE, find a way to execute the Python script. Typically, there's a "Run" or "Execute" option in the menu or a keyboard shortcut (e.g., F5).

- You should see the output, "Hello, World!" printed in the terminal or console.

Learn Python Syntax:

- Python has a straightforward and readable syntax. Familiarize yourself with Python's core concepts, including variables, data types, control structures (e.g., if statements and loops), functions, and classes. Online tutorials, courses, and Python documentation are great resources for learning Python.

Practice and Experiment:

- To become proficient in Python, practice writing code regularly and experiment with different Python features and libraries. You can find Python exercises and coding challenges online to help reinforce your skills.

Use Libraries and Modules:

- Python has a vast ecosystem of libraries and modules that extend its functionality for various purposes. You can use libraries like NumPy for numerical computing, pandas for data manipulation, Matplotlib for data visualization, and more. Install these libraries using the package manager pip (e.g., pip install numpy).

Debugging:

- Learn how to debug your code using tools provided by your code editor or IDE. Debugging helps you find and fix errors in your programs.

Documentation and Community:

- Python has extensive documentation available online (docs.python.org). When you encounter problems or have questions, the Python community is also an excellent resource. Websites like Stack Overflow and the Python subreddit are great places to seek help and advice.

Version Control:

- Consider using version control systems like Git to manage your code. This allows you to track changes, collaborate with others, and revert to previous versions if needed.

Advanced Topics:

- As you gain experience, explore more advanced Python topics, such as object-oriented programming, file handling, web development with frameworks like Flask or Django, data science, machine learning, and automation.

Programming with Python is an enjoyable and rewarding experience, especially for beginners. Start with simple projects and gradually work your way up to more complex applications as you become more comfortable with the language and its features.

Creating a simple python program with steps

Open a Text Editor:

- Open a text editor of your choice. As mentioned earlier, you can use Notepad, TextEdit, Visual Studio Code, Sublime Text, or any other code editor.

Write Python Code:

- In the text editor, write the following Python code:

```python
# This is a comment. It won't be executed by Python.
# We're going to calculate the area of a rectangle.

# Input: Length and width of the rectangle from the user
```

```python
length = float(input("Enter the
length of the rectangle: "))
width = float(input("Enter the
width of the rectangle: "))

# Calculate the area
area = length * width

# Output the result
print(f"The area of the
rectangle is {area} square
units.")
```

In this code:

- We start with comments (lines starting with #) to explain what the code does. Comments are for human readability and are ignored by Python.
- We use the input function to get the length and width of the rectangle from the user. input returns a string, so we use float() to convert the input to floating-point numbers.

- We calculate the area by multiplying the length and width.
- We use the print function to display the result to the user, formatted as a string.

Save the File:

- Save the file with a .py extension, such as `rectangle_area.py`.

Run the Python Program:

- Open a terminal or command prompt.
- Navigate to the directory where your Python file is saved using the cd command.
- Run the program using:

```
python rectangle_area.py
```
or
```
python3 rectangle_area.py
```

Provide User Input:

- When you run the program, it will prompt you to enter the length and width of the rectangle. Input these values, e.g., 5 for length and 3 for width, and press Enter.

View the Output:

- The program will calculate the area (in this case, 5 * 3 = 15) and display the result:

The area of the rectangle is 15.0 square units.

You have now created a simple Python program that calculates the area of a rectangle based on user input. This example illustrates the process of creating a Python program, obtaining user input, performing calculations, and displaying the result. Feel free to modify and expand upon this code as you continue to learn Python programming.

How to program with Java

Programming with Java involves several steps, from setting up your development environment to writing and executing Java code. Here's a step-by-step guide on how to get started with programming in Java:

Install Java Development Kit (JDK):

- Java requires the Java Development Kit (JDK) to be installed on your computer. You can download the latest JDK version from the official Oracle website or choose an open-source alternative like OpenJDK.

Set Up Your Development Environment:

- Choose an Integrated Development Environment (IDE) for Java programming. Some popular Java IDEs include Eclipse, IntelliJ IDEA, and NetBeans. Install your chosen IDE.

Create a Java Project:

- Open your IDE and create a new Java project. Give your project a name, and choose the appropriate JDK version.

Write Java Code:

- In your Java project, create a new Java class. A Java class is where you write your code.
- Write your Java code within the class. Here's a simple "Hello, World!" example:

```java
public class HelloWorld {
    public static void
main(String[] args) {

System.out.println("Hello,
World!");
    }
}
```

In this code:

- public class HelloWorld declares a class named HelloWorld.

- public static void main(String[] args) is the main method, which is the entry point of the program.
- System.out.println("Hello, World!"); prints "Hello, World!" to the console.

Compile the Java Code:

- Most Java IDEs automatically compile your code. However, if you're not using an IDE, you can compile your Java code using the javac command from the command line. For example:

```
javac HelloWorld.java
```

This command generates a bytecode file with a .class extension.

Run the Java Program:

- In your IDE, you can run the Java program by clicking a "Run" button or using a keyboard shortcut. If you're using the command line, use the java command to execute the program:

java HelloWorld

You should see the output, "Hello, World!" printed to the console.

Learn Java Syntax:

- Familiarize yourself with Java's syntax and core concepts. Study topics such as variables, data types, control structures (e.g., if statements and loops), methods, and classes. Online tutorials, courses, and Java documentation can help you learn Java programming.

Practice and Experiment:

- Practice writing Java code regularly and experiment with different Java features and libraries. Solve programming challenges and work on small projects to gain experience.

Use Libraries and Frameworks:

- Java has a vast ecosystem of libraries and frameworks for various purposes. Explore libraries like Apache Commons, Hibernate for database access, Spring for building web applications, and more.

Debugging:

- Learn how to debug your Java code using tools provided by your IDE or use the System.out.println() method to print values and debug your code manually.

Documentation and Community:

- Java has comprehensive documentation available on the Oracle website. When you encounter problems or have questions, the Java community is also a valuable resource. Websites like Stack Overflow and Java forums can provide assistance.

Advanced Topics:

- As you gain proficiency in Java, delve into advanced topics such as object-oriented programming, JavaFX for desktop applications, Java EE for enterprise applications, and Android app development using Java.

Programming with Java offers a wide range of possibilities, from developing desktop and web applications to working with large-scale enterprise systems. By following these steps and continuously learning and practicing, you can become a proficient Java programmer.

Creating a simple java program with steps
Here's a step-by-step guide:

Install Java Development Kit (JDK):

- Make sure you have the Java Development Kit (JDK) installed on your computer. You can download it from the official Oracle website or use an open-source alternative like OpenJDK.

Set Up Your Development Environment:

- Choose an Integrated Development Environment (IDE) for Java programming. For this example, we'll use the Eclipse IDE. Download and install Eclipse if you haven't already.

Create a New Java Project:

- Open Eclipse and create a new Java project:
    - Click on "File" > "New" > "Java Project."
    - Give your project a name, e.g., "SimpleCalculator."
    - Click "Finish" to create the project.

Create a Java Class:

- Inside your project, create a new Java class:
  - Right-click on the "src" folder in your project.
  - Choose "New" > "Class."
  - Name your class, e.g., "Calculator."
  - Check the box that says "public static void main(String[] args)."
  - Click "Finish."

Write Java Code:

- In your newly created class (Calculator.java), write the Java code for the program:

```java
import java.util.Scanner;

public class Calculator {
    public static void
main(String[] args) {
        // Create a Scanner
object for user input
        Scanner scanner = new
Scanner(System.in);
```

```java
        // Prompt the user to enter two numbers
        System.out.print("Enter the first number: ");
        double num1 = scanner.nextDouble();

        System.out.print("Enter the second number: ");
        double num2 = scanner.nextDouble();

        // Calculate the sum of the two numbers
        double sum = num1 + num2;

        // Display the result
        System.out.println("The sum of " + num1 + " and " + num2 + " is: " + sum);

        // Close the scanner
```

```java
        scanner.close();
    }
}
```

In this code:
- We import the java.util.Scanner
  class to read user input.
- We create a Scanner object
  named scanner to read user
  input from the console.
- We prompt the user to enter two
  numbers, read them using
  scanner.nextDouble(), calculate
  their sum, and display the result.

Compile and Run the Java Program:
- Save your Java file.
- Right-click on the Calculator
  class in the Eclipse IDE.
- Select "Run As" > "Java
  Application."

Provide User Input:
- When you run the program, it
  will prompt you to enter two
  numbers. Input the numbers
  and press Enter.

View the Output:

- The program will calculate the sum of the numbers and display the result in the console.

Congratulations! You've successfully created and run a simple Java program. This example illustrates the process of setting up a Java development environment, writing Java code, compiling it, and executing it. You can expand on this code and explore more advanced Java programming concepts as you continue to learn Java.

How to program with C#

Creating a C# program involves several steps, from setting up your development environment to writing, compiling, and running C# code. Here's a step-by-step guide to getting started with C# programming:

Install Visual Studio (Optional but recommended):

- Visual Studio is a popular integrated development environment (IDE) for C# programming. You can download the free Community edition of Visual Studio from the official Microsoft website. Alternatively, you can use Visual Studio Code (VS Code), a lightweight code editor, along with the C# extension.

Create a New C# Project (Visual Studio):

- If you're using Visual Studio, follow these steps:
    - Open Visual Studio.
    - Click on "File" > "New" > "Project."
    - In the "Create a new project" dialog, select "Console App (.NET Core)" or "Console App (.NET Framework)"

depending on your preference.

- Choose a project name and location, and click "Create."

Write C# Code:

- In your C# project, you'll find a file with the extension .cs (e.g., Program.cs). This is the main code file.
- Write your C# code inside the Main method. Here's a simple "Hello, World!" example:

```csharp
using System;

class Program
{
    static void Main()
    {

Console.WriteLine("Hello,
World!");
    }
```

}

In this code:

- We include the using System; directive to access the Console class for output.
- We declare a class named Program.
- Inside the class, we define the Main method, which is the entry point of the program.
- We use Console.WriteLine to print "Hello, World!" to the console.

Compile and Run (Visual Studio):

- If you're using Visual Studio, you can simply click the "Start" button (or press F5) to build and run your C# program.
- You should see the output, "Hello, World!" displayed in the console.

Create a New C# Project (Visual Studio Code):

- If you're using Visual Studio Code, follow these steps:
    - Open Visual Studio Code.
    - Install the C# extension if you haven't already (search for "C#" in the Extensions sidebar).
    - Create a new folder for your project and open it in VS Code.
    - In the terminal, run the following command to create a new C# console application:

dotnet new console -n MyCSharpApp
    - Replace "MyCSharpApp" with your desired project name.

Write C# Code (Visual Studio Code):
    - Open the generated .cs file (e.g., Program.cs) in the editor.
    - Write your C# code inside the Main method, similar to the previous example.

Compile and Run (Visual Studio
Code):

- In the terminal, navigate to your project folder.
- Run the following command to build and run your C# program:

```
dotnet run
```

You should see the output, "Hello, World!" displayed in the terminal.

This guide covers the basics of setting up a C# development environment, writing code, and running a C# application. You can now explore more advanced C# programming concepts and create more complex C# applications as you continue to learn.

Creating a simple C# program

Let's create a simple C# program that calculates the sum of two numbers and displays the result. I'll provide step-by-step instructions along with explanations of each part of the code.

Set Up Your Development Environment:

- You can use Visual Studio or Visual Studio Code for C# programming. In this example, we'll use Visual Studio Code along with the .NET Core SDK.

Create a New C# Console Application:

- Open your terminal or command prompt.
- Navigate to the directory where you want to create your project.
- Run the following command to create a new C# console application: dotnet new console -n SimpleCalculator
- This command creates a new folder named "SimpleCalculator" and generates a basic C# console application within it.

Open the C# Project in Visual Studio Code:

- Navigate to the project folder:cd SimpleCalculator
-
- Open the project in Visual Studio Code: code .
-

Edit the C# Code:

- In Visual Studio Code, open the Program.cs file located inside the "SimpleCalculator" folder.
- Replace the existing code with the following code:

```csharp
using System;

class Program
{
    static void Main()
    {
        // Prompt the user to enter two numbers
        Console.Write("Enter the first number: ");
```

```csharp
        double num1 =
Convert.ToDouble(Console.ReadLin
e());

        Console.Write("Enter the
second number: ");
        double num2 =
Convert.ToDouble(Console.ReadLin
e());

        // Calculate the sum of
the two numbers
        double sum = num1 +
num2;

        // Display the result
        Console.WriteLine($"The
sum of {num1} and {num2} is:
{sum}");
    }
}
```

In this code:

- We include the using System; directive to access standard input and output functionality.
- Inside the Main method, we:
    - Prompt the user to enter two numbers using Console.Write and read their input with Console.ReadLine().
    - Convert the user input to double using Convert.ToDouble().
    - Calculate the sum of the two numbers.
    - Display the result using Console.WriteLine().

Compile and Run the C# Program:

- In the terminal, while inside the project folder, run the following command to build and run the program:

```
dotnet run
```

-

- You'll be prompted to enter two numbers.
- After entering the numbers, the program will calculate and display the sum.

Enter the first number: 10.5
Enter the second number: 20.3
The sum of 10.5 and 20.3 is: 30.8
This example demonstrates how to set up a C# development environment, write code, compile, and execute a C# application. You can use this as a starting point to explore more advanced C# programming concepts and create more complex C# applications.

How to program with Ruby

Programming with Ruby involves a series of steps, from setting up your development environment to writing and running Ruby code. Ruby is known for its simplicity and readability, making it an excellent choice for both beginners and experienced programmers. Here's a step-by-step guide on how to get started with programming in Ruby:

Install Ruby:

- First, you need to ensure that Ruby is installed on your computer. You can download the latest version of Ruby from the official website (https://www.ruby-lang.org/en/documentation/installation/) or use a version manager like RVM (Ruby Version Manager) or rbenv, which allows you to manage multiple Ruby versions on your system.

Set Up a Text Editor:

- Choose a text editor or integrated development environment (IDE) for Ruby programming. You can use basic text editors like Notepad (on Windows) or TextEdit (on macOS) or opt for code editors/IDEs like Visual Studio

Code, Sublime Text, Atom, RubyMine, or others. Install your chosen editor/IDE.

Write Your First Ruby Program:

- Open your text editor or IDE and create a new file with a .rb extension. For example, you can name the file hello.rb.
- Write your Ruby code. Here's a simple "Hello, World!" program:

```ruby
puts "Hello, World!"
```

In this code:

- puts is a method used to print text to the console.
- "Hello, World!" is the text you want to display.

Save the Ruby File:

- Save the file with a .rb extension (e.g., hello.rb) to a directory of your choice.

Run Your Ruby Program:

- Open a terminal or command prompt on your computer.

- Navigate to the directory where you saved your Ruby file using the cd command. For example:

```
cd path/to/your/directory
```

- Execute the Ruby program using the ruby command followed by the name of your Ruby file:

```
ruby hello.rb
```

- You should see the output, "Hello, World!" displayed in the terminal.

Learn Ruby Syntax and Concepts:

- Familiarize yourself with Ruby's syntax and core concepts, including variables, data types, control structures (e.g., if statements and loops), methods, and classes. Online tutorials, courses, and the official Ruby documentation are valuable resources for learning Ruby.

Practice and Experiment:

- Practice writing Ruby code regularly and experiment with different Ruby features. Solve coding challenges and work on small projects to gain experience.

Use Ruby Gems:

- Ruby has a rich ecosystem of libraries called "gems." You can use the package manager gem to install and manage Ruby gems. Explore gems for various purposes, such as web development, data analysis, and more.

Documentation and Community:

- Ruby has comprehensive documentation available online. When you encounter problems or have questions, the Ruby community is a helpful resource. Websites like Stack Overflow and Ruby forums are great places to seek assistance.

Advanced Topics:

- As you become more proficient in Ruby, delve into advanced topics such as object-oriented programming, web development using Ruby on Rails, database access, and automation scripts.

Programming with Ruby offers a straightforward and enjoyable experience. By following these steps and continuing to explore Ruby's capabilities, you can become a proficient Ruby programmer.

Creating a simple C# program

Let's create a simple Ruby program that calculates the area of a rectangle based on user input. I'll guide you through each step, and I'll explain the code as we go along.

Set Up Your Ruby Environment:

- Ensure that you have Ruby installed on your computer. You can check if Ruby is installed by opening a terminal or command prompt and running the following command:

```
ruby --version
```

If Ruby is not installed, download and install it from the official Ruby website (https://www.ruby-lang.org/en/documentation/installation/) or use a version manager like RVM (Ruby Version Manager).

Create a Ruby File:

- Open a text editor or code editor of your choice (e.g., Visual Studio Code, Sublime Text, or Atom).
- Create a new file and save it with a .rb extension, such as rectangle_area.rb.

Write Your Ruby Code:

- In your Ruby file (rectangle_area.rb), write the following Ruby code:

```
# This program calculates the
area of a rectangle.
```

```ruby
# Prompt the user for input
print "Enter the length of the
rectangle: "
length = gets.chomp.to_f

print "Enter the width of the
rectangle: "
width = gets.chomp.to_f

# Calculate the area
area = length * width

# Display the result
puts "The area of the rectangle
is #{area} square units."
```

In this code:

- We use print to display messages to the user without a newline character.
- gets.chomp is used to get user input and remove the newline character at the end of the input.

- We convert the user input to floating-point numbers using to_f.
- We calculate the area of the rectangle by multiplying the length and width.
- puts is used to display the result to the user.

Run Your Ruby Program:

- Open a terminal or command prompt.
- Navigate to the directory where you saved your Ruby file using the cd command.
- Run the Ruby program using the following command:

```
ruby rectangle_area.rb
```

Provide User Input:

- When you run the program, it will prompt you to enter the length and width of the rectangle. Input these values

(e.g., 5 for length and 3 for width) and press Enter.
View the Output:

- The program will calculate the area (in this case, 5 * 3 = 15) and display the result:

Enter the length of the rectangle: 5
Enter the width of the rectangle: 3
The area of the rectangle is 15.0 square units.

This example demonstrates the process of setting up a Ruby development environment, writing Ruby code, and executing a Ruby script. You can use this as a foundation to explore more advanced Ruby programming concepts and create more complex Ruby applications.

How to program with Swift

Programming with Swift, a powerful and easy-to-learn language developed by Apple, allows you to build applications for iOS, macOS, watchOS, tvOS, and more. Here's a step-by-step guide on how to get started with programming in Swift:

Set Up Your Development Environment:

- Install Xcode: Xcode is the official integrated development environment (IDE) for Swift and iOS/macOS app development. It includes the Swift compiler and a rich set of tools for building, debugging, and testing your apps. You can download Xcode for free from the Mac App Store.

Create a New Swift Project:

- Open Xcode.
- Click on "File" > "New" > "Project."
- Choose the template that best suits your project type (e.g., "iOS App," "macOS App," etc.).
- Click "Next" and provide the necessary project details (e.g., product name, organization identifier).

- Choose a location to save your project and click "Create."

Write Swift Code:

- In Xcode, you'll see a file named "ViewController.swift" (for iOS) or a similar file with a .swift extension (e.g., "AppDelegate.swift" for macOS). This is where you'll write your Swift code.
- In the default template, you'll find a basic Swift program in the view controller or app delegate file. You can modify this code or start from scratch.

Learn Swift Syntax and Concepts:

- Swift has a clean and expressive syntax. Familiarize yourself with Swift's key concepts, including variables, data types, control structures (e.g., if statements and loops), functions, and classes. Online tutorials, courses, and Apple's Swift documentation are excellent resources for learning Swift.

Practice and Experiment:

- Practice writing Swift code regularly and experiment with different Swift features. Building small projects or iOS/macOS apps is a great way to gain experience.

Use Swift Frameworks and Libraries:

- Swift has a variety of frameworks and libraries for various purposes. For iOS/macOS app development, explore UIKit (for user interfaces) and other iOS/macOS-specific libraries. For server-side development, you can use the Vapor framework, among others.

Documentation and Community:

- The Swift community is active, and there are many resources available online. Apple's Swift documentation, forums like Stack Overflow, and various Swift-focused websites and communities are excellent places to seek help and share knowledge.

Advanced Topics:

- As you become more comfortable with Swift, delve into advanced topics like protocol-oriented programming, data persistence, working with APIs, and using Core Data for iOS/macOS app development.

Build and Test Your App:

- Use Xcode to build, test, and run your Swift app. You can run your app in the simulator for testing or deploy it to a physical device (e.g., iPhone or iPad) for real-world testing.

Publish Your App:

- If you're building an iOS or macOS app, you can publish it to

the App Store or Mac App Store once it's complete. Follow Apple's guidelines for app submission and review.
Continuously Learn and Explore:

- The field of app development and Swift programming is constantly evolving. Stay updated with the latest Swift features and best practices by reading blogs, attending conferences, and participating in online Swift communities.

Programming with Swift is a rewarding experience, and it enables you to create applications for Apple's diverse ecosystem of devices. By following these steps and continuously learning and practicing, you can become a proficient Swift programmer.

Creating a simple Swift program

Let's create a simple Swift program that converts temperatures between Celsius and Fahrenheit. Here are the steps:

Set Up Your Development Environment:

- Ensure that you have Xcode installed on your computer, as mentioned in the previous example.

Create a New Swift Project:

- Open Xcode.
- Click on "File" > "New" > "Project..."
- Select "Command Line Tool" under the "macOS" section.
- Click "Next."
- Provide a name for your project (e.g., "TemperatureConverter").
- Choose a location to save your project.
- Ensure that the language is set to "Swift."
- Click "Next" and then "Create."

Write Swift Code:

- In Xcode, open the Swift file with a .swift extension (e.g., "main.swift").
- Replace the default code with the following Swift code:

```swift
// This program converts temperatures between Celsius and Fahrenheit.

func celsiusToFahrenheit(celsius: Double) -> Double {
    return (celsius * 9/5) + 32
}

func fahrenheitToCelsius(fahrenheit: Double) -> Double {
    return (fahrenheit - 32) * 5/9
}

// Prompt the user for input
```

```swift
print("Choose an option:")
print("1. Convert from Celsius
to Fahrenheit")
print("2. Convert from
Fahrenheit to Celsius")

let choice = readLine()

if let choice = choice, let
option = Int(choice) {
    switch option {
    case 1:
        print("Enter temperature
in Celsius:")
        if let celsiusInput =
readLine(), let celsius =
Double(celsiusInput) {
            let fahrenheit =
celsiusToFahrenheit(celsius:
celsius)
            print("Temperature
in Fahrenheit: \(fahrenheit)°F")
        } else {
```

```swift
                print("Invalid
input.")
            }
    case 2:
        print("Enter temperature
in Fahrenheit:")
        if let fahrenheitInput =
readLine(), let fahrenheit =
Double(fahrenheitInput) {
            let celsius =
fahrenheitToCelsius(fahrenheit:
fahrenheit)
            print("Temperature
in Celsius: \(celsius)°C")
        } else {
            print("Invalid
input.")
        }
    default:
        print("Invalid choice.")
    }
} else {
    print("Invalid choice.")
}
```

In this code:
- We define two functions, celsiusToFahrenheit and fahrenheitToCelsius, to perform temperature conversions.
- We use print to display a menu of options to the user.
- We use readLine() to read the user's choice.
- Depending on the user's choice, we prompt them to enter a temperature value and perform the conversion.

Run Your Swift Program:
- In Xcode, press the "Run" button or use the shortcut Cmd + R.

Provide User Input:
- The program will run in the console and display a menu.
- Choose option 1 or 2 to convert temperatures.
- Enter the temperature value when prompted.

View the Output:
- The program will perform the conversion and display the result.

Here's an example of the program in action:

```
Choose an option:
1. Convert from Celsius to
Fahrenheit
2. Convert from Fahrenheit to
Celsius
1
Enter temperature in Celsius:
25
Temperature in Fahrenheit:
77.0°F
```

This example demonstrates how to create a command-line program in Swift and interact with the user to perform conversions.

Low-level programming languages, such as Assembly language and machine code, play a crucial role in computer systems and software development for several important reasons:

Direct Hardware Interaction: Low-level languages allow programmers to interact directly with the hardware of a computer. This level of control is essential for tasks like writing device drivers, operating system components, and embedded systems programming, where precision and efficiency are critical.

Efficiency: Low-level languages offer fine-grained control over hardware resources, which allows programmers to optimize code for performance and memory usage. This is especially important in applications where speed and efficiency are paramount, such as real-time systems and game development.

Portability: Code written in low-level languages is often highly portable across different hardware architectures. While high-level languages abstract away hardware details, low-level languages can be adapted to various platforms with relatively minor modifications, making them suitable for cross-platform development.

Real-Time Systems: Low-level programming is essential for real-time systems, where precise timing and responsiveness are necessary. Examples include avionics systems, medical devices, robotics, and industrial automation.

Security: In security-related applications, like cryptography and secure communications, low-level programming allows for fine-grained control over memory and execution, reducing the risk of vulnerabilities and exploits.

Resource-Constrained Environments: Low-level languages are often used in resource-constrained environments, such as embedded systems and IoT

devices. They enable programmers to maximize the utilization of limited memory and processing power.
Operating Systems Development: The core components of operating systems, including kernels and device drivers, are typically written in low-level languages. These components manage hardware resources, memory, and system processes, requiring the level of control offered by low-level languages.
Learn How Computers Work: Learning and working with low-level languages provide a deep understanding of how computers function at the hardware level. This knowledge is valuable for systems programming, debugging, and optimizing code written in high-level languages.
Legacy Code: Some legacy systems and applications are written in low-level languages. Knowledge of

these languages is necessary for maintaining and extending such systems.

Low-Level Hardware Manipulation: Low-level languages allow direct manipulation of hardware registers and memory addresses, which is essential for tasks like signal processing and controlling hardware components in embedded systems.

Reverse Engineering: In security analysis and reverse engineering of software and hardware, knowledge of low-level languages is crucial for understanding and analyzing binary code and proprietary protocols.

While low-level programming languages offer many advantages, they also come with challenges, such as increased development time, complexity, and a steeper learning curve. Programmers need to weigh the benefits and trade-offs of using low-level languages based on the specific requirements of their projects. In many cases, a combination of low-level and high-level languages is employed to achieve the best balance between performance and productivity.

Examples of low-level programming languages and their specific functions: Low-level programming languages provide a high degree of control over hardware and system resources. Here are some examples of low-level programming languages and their specific functions:

Assembly Language:

- Specific Function: Assembly language is a low-level language that is specific to a particular computer architecture or microprocessor. Programmers write code using mnemonics and symbols that correspond directly to machine code instructions.
- Use Cases: Assembly language is often used for tasks that require direct control over hardware, such as writing device drivers,

embedded systems programming, and optimizing critical sections of code.

Machine Code:

- **Specific Function:** Machine code is the lowest-level programming language, consisting of binary or hexadecimal instructions that can be executed directly by a computer's central processing unit (CPU).
- **Use Cases:** Machine code is used in situations where absolute control over hardware is necessary, such as when developing BIOS firmware or bootloaders.

C/C++ with Inline Assembly:

- **Specific Function:** C and C++ programming languages can be used in combination with inline assembly code to achieve low-level control over specific operations. Inline assembly allows the direct insertion of assembly instructions within C/C++ code.

- **Use Cases:** Inline assembly is useful when optimizing critical sections of code or when interfacing with hardware in a low-level manner.

VHDL and Verilog:

- **Specific Function:** VHDL (VHSIC Hardware Description Language) and Verilog are hardware description languages used for designing and simulating digital circuits and systems at the register-transfer level (RTL).

- **Use Cases:** VHDL and Verilog are primarily used in the field of digital design for creating FPGA (Field-Programmable Gate Array) and ASIC (Application-Specific Integrated Circuit) designs, including

custom hardware accelerators
and digital signal processing.
Embedded C:
- Specific Function: Embedded C
  is a variant of the C
  programming language tailored
  for embedded systems
  programming. It provides
  low-level access to hardware
  peripherals and memory
  management.
- Use Cases: Embedded C is used
  extensively in the development
  of firmware for microcontrollers,
  real-time operating systems
  (RTOS), and embedded systems
  in various industries, including
  automotive, IoT, and consumer
  electronics.

FORTRAN (in certain contexts):
- Specific Function: While
  FORTRAN is generally
  considered a high-level
  language, it can be used in a

low-level manner for numerical and scientific computing. Programmers can optimize code to operate close to the hardware for maximum performance.

- Use Cases: FORTRAN is commonly used in scientific and engineering applications where performance is critical, such as simulations and weather modeling.

SIMD (Single Instruction, Multiple Data) Assembly Languages:

- Specific Function: SIMD assembly languages, such as Intel's x86 assembly with SSE (Streaming SIMD Extensions), are designed for parallel processing of data elements. They provide direct control over vectorized instructions for tasks like multimedia processing and scientific computation.

- Use Cases: SIMD assembly is used to accelerate tasks that can be parallelized, such as image and video processing, 3D graphics rendering, and scientific simulations.

These low-level programming languages are tailored to specific needs where precise control over hardware resources, performance optimization, and direct manipulation of hardware components are essential requirements. Programmers often use them in conjunction with high-level languages to strike a balance between control and productivity.

How to program with Assembly Language

Programming in Assembly Language involves writing code that directly corresponds to machine code instructions for a specific computer architecture or microprocessor. Assembly language is a low-level programming language, and writing assembly code provides a deep level of control over a computer's hardware. Here are the general steps to get started with programming in Assembly Language:

Choose a Target Architecture:

- Assembly language is highly architecture-specific, meaning that you need to choose the specific computer architecture or microprocessor you want to program for. Popular architectures include x86, ARM, MIPS, and more.

Set Up a Development Environment:

- To write, assemble, and test assembly code, you'll need a development environment that includes an assembler, debugger, and text editor. Depending on your target architecture, you might use different tools. Here are some common ones:

- x86 (Intel/AMD): NASM (Netwide Assembler) or MASM (Microsoft Macro Assembler) for Windows development.
- ARM: ARM Assembly with GNU Assembler (GAS) or Keil's ARM Development Tools.
- MIPS: MARS (MIPS Assembler and Runtime Simulator).

Learn Assembly Language Basics:

- Familiarize yourself with the assembly language syntax, which varies depending on the architecture. You'll need to understand concepts like registers, instructions, memory addressing modes, and conditional branches.
- Study the instruction set architecture (ISA) documentation for your target

architecture. This documentation defines the available instructions, their opcodes, and their effects on registers and memory.

Write Assembly Code:

- Use a text editor to write your assembly code. Save the code with an appropriate file extension (e.g., .asm for NASM or .s for GAS).
- Write code that consists of mnemonics (e.g., mov, add, jmp) and operands (registers, memory addresses, constants) to perform specific tasks.

Assemble the Code:

- Use the assembler provided by your development environment to convert your assembly code into machine code. This step generates an executable file or binary output.

Debug Your Code:

- Debugging assembly code can be challenging. Use the debugger included in your development environment to step through the code, set breakpoints, inspect registers and memory, and identify and fix errors.

Test Your Code:

- Test your assembly code thoroughly to ensure that it behaves as expected. This may involve writing test cases, running simulations, and monitoring the program's behavior.

Optimize for Performance (Optional):

- Assembly language allows for fine-grained control over performance. You can optimize your code by minimizing instruction count, reducing memory access latency, and exploiting parallelism in the architecture.

Document Your Code:

- Assembly code can be cryptic, so thorough comments and documentation are essential for understanding and maintaining the code. Document the purpose of each section, the role of specific registers, and the overall algorithm.

Backup and Version Control:

- Keep backups of your assembly code, and consider using version control systems like Git to track changes and collaborate with others.

Explore Advanced Topics (Optional):

- As you become more proficient in assembly programming, you can explore advanced topics like interrupt handling, operating system development, and writing device drivers.

Practice and Learn:

- Assembly programming is a skill that improves with practice. Work on increasingly complex projects and study existing assembly code to learn new techniques and strategies.

Remember that programming in Assembly Language can be challenging due to its low-level nature and architecture-specific syntax. However, it provides unparalleled control over hardware and can be highly rewarding for tasks where efficiency and precise control are essential.

Creating a simple Assembly Language program

Let's create a simple Assembly Language program for the x86 architecture that calculates the sum of two numbers entered by the user. I'll provide an example using NASM (Netwide Assembler), which is a popular assembler for x86 assembly programming. We'll focus on Linux as the target platform.

Here's a step-by-step guide on how to create and run the program:

Install NASM (if not already installed):

- You can install NASM on Linux using the package manager. For example, on Ubuntu, you can use:

```
sudo apt-get install nasm
```

-

Create an Assembly File:

- Open a text editor and create a new file named sum.asm. This will be your assembly source code file.

Write Assembly Code:

- Open sum.asm and write the following assembly code:

```
section .data
    prompt db "Enter the first number: ", 0
```

```nasm
    prompt2 db "Enter the second
number: ", 0
    result db "The sum is: ", 0
    format db "%d", 0

section .bss
    num1 resb 10
    num2 resb 10
    sum resb 10

section .text
    global _start

_start:
    ; Display prompt and read
the first number
    mov eax, 4
    mov ebx, 1
    mov ecx, prompt
    mov edx, 23
    int 0x80
    mov eax, 3
    mov ebx, 0
    mov ecx, num1
```

```
        mov edx, 10
        int 0x80

        ; Display prompt2 and read
the second number
    mov eax, 4
    mov ebx, 1
    mov ecx, prompt2
    mov edx, 24
    int 0x80
    mov eax, 3
    mov ebx, 0
    mov ecx, num2
    mov edx, 10
    int 0x80

        ; Convert num1 and num2 to
integers
    mov eax, 0
    mov esi, num1
    call atoi
    mov ebx, eax
    mov eax, 0
    mov esi, num2
```

```nasm
    call atoi

    ; Calculate the sum
    add eax, ebx

    ; Convert the sum to a
string
    mov esi, eax
    mov edi, sum
    call itoa

    ; Display the result
    mov eax, 4
    mov ebx, 1
    mov ecx, result
    mov edx, 13
    int 0x80
    mov eax, 4
    mov ebx, 1
    mov ecx, sum
    mov edx, 10
    int 0x80

    ; Exit the program
```

```nasm
        mov eax, 1
        mov ebx, 0
        int 0x80

atoi:
    ; Code for converting ASCII
to integer (atoi)
    ; Input: ESI - Pointer to
the ASCII string
    ; Output: EAX - Integer
value
    xor eax, eax
    xor ecx, ecx

atoi_loop:
        mov cl, byte [esi]
        cmp cl, 0
        je atoi_done

        sub cl, '0'
        imul eax, eax, 10
        add eax, ecx
        inc esi
        jmp atoi_loop
```

```asm
atoi_done:
    ret

itoa:
    ; Code for converting
integer to ASCII (itoa)
    ; Input: ESI - Integer value
    ; Output: EDI - Pointer to
the ASCII string
    xor ecx, ecx
    mov ebx, 10

itoa_loop:
    xor edx, edx
    div ebx
    add dl, '0'
    dec edi
    mov [edi], dl
    test eax, eax
    jnz itoa_loop

    ret
```

This assembly program does the following:

- Displays prompts and reads two numbers from the user.
- Converts the input ASCII strings to integers.
- Calculates the sum.
- Converts the sum to an ASCII string.
- Displays the result.

Assemble and Link the Program:

- Open your terminal and navigate to the directory containing sum.asm.
- Use NASM to assemble the code and link it with ld:

```
nasm -f elf sum.asm -o sum.o
ld sum.o -m elf_i386 -s -o sum
```

-

Run the Program:

- Run the program by executing the sum binary:

```
./sum
```

-

- The program will prompt you to enter two numbers, calculate their sum, and display the result.

This example demonstrates the basic structure of an x86 assembly program and how to perform input, calculations, and output. Assembly programming can be challenging, but it provides a high level of control over system resources and is valuable for systems programming and optimization.

How to program with Machine Code

Programming in machine code involves writing instructions in the form of binary code that can be executed directly by a computer's central processing unit (CPU). Machine code is the lowest-level programming language and is highly architecture-specific. Here's a general overview of how to program in machine code:

Understand the Architecture:

- Machine code is specific to a particular computer architecture or microprocessor. You need a deep understanding of the target architecture's instruction set, memory organization, and I/O operations. Common architectures include x86, ARM, MIPS, and more.

Set Up a Development Environment:

- You'll need a development environment that allows you to create and execute machine code. This typically includes an assembler, a disassembler, a text editor, and an emulator or hardware for testing. Tools like assemblers and emulators vary depending on the architecture you're targeting.

Learn the Instruction Set:

- Study the documentation for the target architecture's instruction set. This documentation provides details about the available instructions, their opcodes (binary representations), and their effects on registers, memory, and I/O devices.

Write Machine Code:

- Machine code consists of binary instructions that represent operations to be performed by the CPU. Each instruction is represented by a sequence of binary bits, and you'll need to write these instructions manually.
- Use a text editor to write the binary instructions in a human-readable format. It's common to represent each instruction in hexadecimal format for readability.

Assemble the Code:

- Use an assembler to convert your human-readable machine code into binary machine code. The assembler will generate a binary file that can be executed by the target architecture's CPU.
- Assembler directives may be used to specify data sections, labels, and memory locations for instructions.

Test and Debug:

- Testing and debugging machine code can be challenging. Use an emulator or real hardware to execute your code and observe the results.
- Debugging tools for machine code may be limited, so you'll need to rely on techniques like manual inspection of registers and memory.

Optimize for Performance (Optional):

- Machine code allows for low-level optimization. You can

analyze the generated code for opportunities to improve performance by reducing instruction count, minimizing memory access latency, and exploiting parallelism.

Document Your Code:

- Given the cryptic nature of machine code, thorough comments and documentation are essential. Document the purpose of each instruction, the expected behavior, and any data structures.

Backup and Version Control:

- Keep backups of your machine code and consider using version control systems to track changes, especially when working on complex projects.

Practice and Learn:

- Machine code programming is a skill that improves with practice. Work on simple projects, study existing machine code, and gradually tackle more complex tasks.

Programming in machine code is challenging and is typically reserved for tasks that require precise control over hardware resources or for creating low-level system components. Most modern software development is done in higher-level languages, as they offer better productivity and portability. Nonetheless, understanding machine code can be valuable for debugging, reverse engineering, and embedded systems development.

Creating a simple Machine Code program

Creating a simple machine code program is highly dependent on the specific computer architecture you're targeting. Machine code is represented in binary or hexadecimal format, and writing it directly can be extremely challenging and error-prone. Additionally, explaining machine code in

text form can be cumbersome due to the lack of a human-readable syntax.
However, I can provide a basic example in assembly language (which is a more human-readable representation of machine code) and show you how it corresponds to machine code. Let's create a simple program in the x86 assembly language that adds two numbers.

```
section .data
    num1 dd 10  ; Define and
initialize num1 to 10 (32-bit
integer)
    num2 dd 20  ; Define and
initialize num2 to 20 (32-bit
integer)
    result dd 0 ; Define a
variable to store the result
(initialized to 0)

section .text
global _start

_start:
```

```asm
    ; Load num1 into EAX
register
    mov eax, [num1]

    ; Add num2 to EAX
    add eax, [num2]

    ; Store the result in the
result variable
    mov [result], eax

    ; Exit the program
    mov eax, 1          ; syscall
number for exit
    xor ebx, ebx        ; exit
status (0)
    int 0x80            ; invoke
syscall to exit
```

This x86 assembly code does the following:
It defines three variables: num1,
num2, and result.
Loads the value of num1 into the EAX
register.

Adds the value of num2 to EAX.
Stores the result in the result variable.
Exits the program.
Now, let's assemble this code into machine code using an assembler like NASM:

```
nasm -f elf32 add.asm -o add.o
ld -m elf_i386 -s -o add add.o
```

This will create an executable file named add. You can run it to see the result of adding 10 and 20:

```
./add
```

In this example, we've written assembly language code, assembled it into machine code, and executed it to perform a simple addition operation. While this code is in assembly language, it provides an illustration of the process, as creating machine code directly is usually impractical for anything beyond the simplest instructions. Assembly language provides a more human-readable and manageable way to write low-level code.

How to program with VHDL and Verilog

VHDL (VHSIC Hardware Description Language) and Verilog are hardware description languages used for designing and simulating digital circuits and systems, primarily at the register-transfer level (RTL). These languages allow you to describe the behavior and structure of digital circuits, making them essential for hardware design, verification, and synthesis. Here's a general guide on how to program with VHDL and Verilog:

VHDL:

Learn VHDL Basics:
- Familiarize yourself with the basics of VHDL, including syntax, data types, concurrent and sequential statements, and hierarchical design concepts.

Choose a Development Environment:

- Select a VHDL development environment or simulator, such as Xilinx Vivado, ModelSim, or GHDL (an open-source VHDL simulator).

Write VHDL Code:

- Create a new VHDL file with a .vhd extension using a text editor or an integrated development environment (IDE) provided by your chosen tool.
- Write VHDL code to describe your digital circuit's architecture and behavior. Define entities, architectures, and processes.

Simulate Your Design:

- Use the VHDL simulator to perform simulation tests of your design. Simulators allow you to test your VHDL code's functionality and behavior in a virtual environment.

Debug and Verify:

- Debug any issues that arise during simulation. Common debugging tools include waveform viewers, debugging consoles, and debugging IDE features.

Synthesize for Target Hardware (Optional):

- If you intend to implement your design on FPGA or ASIC hardware, use synthesis tools like Xilinx Vivado or Synopsys Design Compiler to convert your VHDL code into a netlist for hardware synthesis.

Implement on FPGA or ASIC (Optional):

- If your goal is to implement your design on hardware, follow the FPGA or ASIC vendor's guidelines for synthesis and place-and-route to generate a bitstream file for programming your target device.

Verilog:

Learn Verilog Basics:

- Begin by understanding Verilog's fundamental concepts, including modules, signals, data types, and concurrency.

Choose a Development Environment:

- Select a Verilog development environment or simulator, such as Xilinx Vivado, ModelSim, or open-source tools like Icarus Verilog.

Write Verilog Code:

- Create a new Verilog file with a .v extension using a text editor or an integrated development environment (IDE).
- Write Verilog code to describe your digital circuit's functionality, including modules, input and output ports, and behavioral logic.

Simulate Your Design:

- Use a Verilog simulator to
  perform simulation tests.
  Verilog simulators allow you to
  verify that your Verilog code
  functions as expected.

Debug and Verify:

- Debug your design during
  simulation, using waveform
  viewers and debugging features
  provided by your chosen
  simulator.

Synthesize for Target Hardware
(Optional):

- If you intend to implement your
  design on FPGA or ASIC
  hardware, use synthesis tools
  like Xilinx Vivado or Synopsys
  Design Compiler to synthesize
  your Verilog code into a netlist
  for hardware synthesis.

Implement on FPGA or ASIC
(Optional):

- If your goal is to deploy your
  design on hardware, follow the

synthesis and implementation
guidelines provided by the FPGA
or ASIC vendor to generate a
bitstream or configuration file
for your target device.

Test on Hardware (Optional):

- Program your FPGA or ASIC
  device with the generated
  bitstream or configuration file to
  test your design on physical
  hardware.

Both VHDL and Verilog are widely used in
the digital design industry. The choice
between them often depends on personal
preference or the design environment you
are working in. Additionally, various coding
styles and methodologies exist for both
languages, so it's beneficial to learn and
adopt industry best practices for clean and
maintainable code.

Creating a simple VHDL and Verilog program

These examples will illustrate how to create a basic 2-input AND gate using both VHDL and Verilog. An AND gate has two inputs (A and B) and one output (Y). The output Y is the logical AND of the inputs A and B.

VHDL Example:

```vhdl
-- Simple 2-input AND gate in VHDL

-- Entity Declaration
entity AND_GATE is
    Port (
        A, B: in std_logic;
        Y: out std_logic
    );
end AND_GATE;

-- Architecture
architecture Behavioral of AND_GATE is
begin
```

```vhdl
    -- AND gate logic
    process(A, B)
    begin
        Y <= A and B;
    end process;
end Behavioral;
```

Here's how this VHDL program works:
- The program defines an entity called AND_GATE, which has two input ports (A and B) and one output port (Y), all of type std_logic.
- In the architecture section, it creates a process that performs the AND operation between inputs A and B and assigns the result to output Y.

Verilog Example:

```verilog
// Simple 2-input AND gate in Verilog

module AND_GATE(
    input A,
    input B,
```

```verilog
    output Y
);

assign Y = A & B;

endmodule
```

Here's how this Verilog program works:

- The program defines a Verilog module named AND_GATE, which takes two inputs (A and B) and produces one output (Y).
- The assign statement directly connects the output Y to the AND operation of inputs A and B.

These examples are basic introductions to VHDL and Verilog. To use these designs, you would typically simulate them using a simulator like ModelSim (for VHDL and Verilog) or Synopsys VCS (for Verilog) and then synthesize them for a specific hardware target, such as an FPGA or ASIC, if desired. Remember that hardware description languages like VHDL and Verilog are often used for more complex digital designs that involve multiple modules, state machines, and hierarchical structures. These examples demonstrate the fundamental concept of creating a basic logic gate.

How to program with Embedded C

Programming with Embedded C involves writing C code for embedded systems, which are specialized computing devices with dedicated functions and constrained resources. Embedded systems can be found in various applications, including microcontrollers, IoT devices, automotive systems, and industrial automation. Here's a step-by-step guide on how to program with Embedded C:

Understand Embedded Systems:

- Gain a solid understanding of embedded systems, including their architecture, constraints (e.g., limited memory and

processing power), and
real-time requirements.

Choose a Microcontroller/Platform:

- Select a microcontroller or embedded platform suitable for your project. Common microcontroller families include Arduino, Raspberry Pi, PIC, STM32, and AVR.

Set Up a Development Environment:

- Install an Integrated Development Environment (IDE) or text editor suitable for embedded C programming. IDEs like Keil, MPLAB X, and PlatformIO are popular choices.

Learn C Programming:

- Ensure you have a good grasp of the C programming language, as embedded C is an extension of standard C. Focus on concepts like data types, pointers, control flow, and functions.

Read the Datasheet:

- Obtain the datasheet and reference manual for your microcontroller. These documents provide essential information about hardware registers, peripherals, and memory-mapped I/O.

Write Embedded C Code:

- Create a new C source code file with a .c extension in your development environment.
- Write C code to interact with the microcontroller's hardware. Use libraries and headers provided by the manufacturer or community to simplify hardware access.

Access Hardware Peripherals:

- Use C code to configure and control hardware peripherals such as GPIO pins, UART, SPI, I2C, ADC, timers, and interrupts.

- Ensure that you read the datasheet to understand register configurations and memory-mapped addresses for these peripherals.

Implement Real-Time Logic:
- For applications with real-time requirements, design and implement real-time logic using timers and interrupts to respond to events or triggers.

Memory Management:
- Be mindful of memory constraints, stack size, and heap usage. Embedded systems often have limited RAM, so efficient memory management is crucial.

Debug and Test:
- Use debugging tools provided by your development environment or external hardware debuggers to identify and resolve issues.
- Test your code incrementally, starting with basic functionality

and gradually adding more
features.

Optimize Code:

- Optimize your code for size and
  performance. Minimize
  unnecessary loops, function
  calls, and memory usage.
  Compiler optimization settings
  can help achieve this.

Document Your Code:

- Document your code thoroughly,
  including comments explaining
  the purpose of functions,
  variables, and hardware
  interactions. Good
  documentation makes
  maintenance and debugging
  easier.

Cross-Compile:

- Compile your C code for the
  target microcontroller
  architecture. The compiler
  generates machine code

compatible with your specific hardware.

Program the Microcontroller:

- Use a programmer or bootloader to upload the compiled code onto the microcontroller's flash memory.

Test on Hardware:

- Verify the functionality of your embedded C code on the actual hardware. Monitor signals and use debugging tools as needed.

Iterate and Refine:

- Iterate on your code as necessary to add features, fix bugs, and optimize performance. The embedded C development process often involves multiple iterations.

Consider Power Management (for battery-powered devices):

- Implement power-saving techniques to maximize battery life, such as sleep modes, clock gating, and low-power peripherals.

Comply with Safety and Standards (if applicable):

- Ensure that your embedded C code complies with relevant safety standards and regulations, especially in safety-critical applications like automotive or medical devices.

Version Control and Backup:

- Use version control systems like Git to track changes in your code and maintain backups.

Embedded C programming requires a combination of C language skills and a deep understanding of hardware. The process may vary slightly depending on the specific microcontroller or platform you're working with, so always refer to the manufacturer's documentation and community resources for guidance.

Creating a simple Embedded C program

Creating a simple Embedded C program involves writing code for a microcontroller or embedded platform to perform a specific task or control hardware peripherals. In this example, I'll provide a basic Embedded C program for an Arduino microcontroller to blink an LED. We'll use the Arduino IDE, which simplifies the development process. Here are the steps to create and upload a simple Embedded C program to an Arduino board:

Set Up the Arduino IDE:
- Install the Arduino IDE from the official Arduino website (https://www.arduino.cc/en/software).
- Connect your Arduino board to your computer via USB.

Create a New Arduino Sketch:
- Open the Arduino IDE and create a new sketch.

Write the Embedded C Code:

```c
// Simple Embedded C program to blink an LED on Arduino
```

```cpp
// Define the LED pin
const int ledPin = 13; // Most
Arduino boards have an LED on
pin 13

// Setup function runs once at
the start
void setup() {
    pinMode(ledPin, OUTPUT); //
Set the LED pin as an output
}

// Loop function runs repeatedly
void loop() {
    digitalWrite(ledPin, HIGH);
// Turn on the LED
    delay(1000);
// Wait for 1 second
    digitalWrite(ledPin, LOW);
// Turn off the LED
    delay(1000);
// Wait for 1 second
}
```

This code defines a program to blink the built-in LED on most Arduino boards.

Compile the Code:

- Click the "Verify" button (checkmark icon) in the Arduino IDE to compile the code.

Upload the Code to the Arduino:

- Connect your Arduino board to your computer via USB if not already connected.
- Select the appropriate board and COM port from the "Tools" menu in the Arduino IDE.
- Click the "Upload" button (right-arrow icon) to upload the compiled code to the Arduino.

Monitor the LED:

- The LED on the Arduino board should start blinking. It turns on for 1 second and then turns off for 1 second, repeating this pattern.

This example serves as a basic introduction to embedded programming with C. For more complex applications, you can add sensors, control motors, or interface with other hardware peripherals. Be sure to refer to the specific documentation and datasheets for your target microcontroller or embedded platform when working on more advanced projects.

How to program with FORTRAN

Programming with FORTRAN (Formula Translation) involves writing code in the FORTRAN programming language. FORTRAN is a high-level language that is particularly well-suited for scientific and engineering applications, especially numerical and computational tasks. Here are the steps to get started with programming in FORTRAN:

Set Up a Development Environment:

- Install a FORTRAN compiler on your computer. Popular

compilers for FORTRAN include
GNU Fortran (gfortran), Intel
Fortran Compiler (ifort), and
IBM XL Fortran Compiler.

- You can download and install
  gfortran for free as part of the
  GCC (GNU Compiler Collection)
  package.

Choose a Text Editor or Integrated
Development Environment (IDE):

- You can write FORTRAN code
  using a plain text editor (e.g.,
  Notepad++, Visual Studio Code,
  or Sublime Text) or use an IDE
  that supports FORTRAN, such
  as Code::Blocks or Microsoft
  Visual Studio with the Intel
  Fortran Compiler.

Learn FORTRAN Syntax and Basics:

- Familiarize yourself with
  FORTRAN's syntax and basic
  language constructs. This
  includes understanding
  variables, data types, loops,

conditional statements, functions, and subroutines.
- FORTRAN uses a fixed-format or free-format syntax, depending on the version (FORTRAN 77 uses fixed format, while later versions support free format).

Write a Simple FORTRAN Program:
- Create a new text file with a .f, .f90, or .f95 extension (e.g., hello.f90).
- Write a simple FORTRAN program, such as the classic "Hello, World!" program:

```
program hello
  write(*,*) 'Hello, World!'
end program hello
```

- Save the file.

Compile the FORTRAN Program:
- Open your command prompt or terminal.

- Navigate to the directory containing your FORTRAN source code.
- Compile the program using the appropriate compiler. For gfortran, you can use the following command:

```
gfortran -o hello hello.f90
```

This command compiles the program into an executable named hello.

Run the Program:

- Execute the compiled program by running the generated executable:

```
./hello
```

You should see the output: "Hello, World!".

Learn More Advanced Features:

- Explore more advanced features of FORTRAN, such as array handling, file I/O, and numerical computing libraries like LAPACK and BLAS.

- Learn about modern FORTRAN standards like Fortran 90, Fortran 95, and Fortran 2003, which introduced significant improvements over earlier versions.

Use Libraries and Resources:

- Utilize external libraries and resources specific to your field of interest. FORTRAN has a rich ecosystem of libraries and resources for various scientific and engineering domains.

Practice and Experiment:

- The best way to become proficient in FORTRAN is to practice by solving real-world problems. Write programs, experiment with code, and build upon your knowledge.

Refer to Documentation:

- Keep the official FORTRAN documentation and tutorials

handy for reference as you work on more complex projects. Programming in FORTRAN can be a valuable skill for scientific and engineering applications, particularly in fields like physics, chemistry, and computational mathematics. It offers a combination of ease of use and high performance, making it a preferred choice for many numerical computations.

Creating a simple FORTRAN program

Let's create a simple FORTRAN program that calculates the sum of two numbers entered by the user. Here's a basic example:

```fortran
program sum_of_numbers
    implicit none
    real :: num1, num2, sum

    ! Prompt the user to enter
the first number
```

```fortran
    write(*,*) 'Enter the first
number: '
    read(*, *) num1

    ! Prompt the user to enter
the second number
    write(*,*) 'Enter the second
number: '
    read(*, *) num2

    ! Calculate the sum
    sum = num1 + num2

    ! Display the result
    write(*,*) 'The sum is: ',
sum

end program sum_of_numbers
```

Here's how this simple FORTRAN program works:

- program sum_of_numbers defines the main program with the name "sum_of_numbers."

- implicit none enforces explicit variable declaration, which is a good practice in modern FORTRAN programming.
- real :: num1, num2, sum declares three real variables: num1, num2, and sum to store the numbers and the sum.
- write(*,*) 'Enter the first number: ' displays a message asking the user to enter the first number.
- read(*, *) num1 reads the first number entered by the user and stores it in the num1 variable.
- Similarly, we prompt the user to enter the second number and read it into the num2 variable.
- sum = num1 + num2 calculates the sum of num1 and num2 and stores it in the sum variable.
- write(*,*) 'The sum is: ', sum displays the result, including the sum.

To run this program:

Save the code above to a file with a .f90 extension, for example, sum_of_numbers.f90.

Open your terminal or command prompt and navigate to the directory containing the FORTRAN file.

Compile the program using a FORTRAN compiler, such as gfortran:

```
gfortran -o sum_program
sum_of_numbers.f90
```

This command will create an executable named sum_program.

Run the program:

```
./sum_program
```

You'll be prompted to enter two numbers, and the program will display their sum.

This simple FORTRAN program demonstrates the basic structure of a FORTRAN program, including input, calculations, and output. FORTRAN uses a straightforward syntax and is well-suited for numerical and scientific computations.

How to program with SIMD

Programming with SIMD (Single Instruction, Multiple Data) involves utilizing processor instructions and parallel processing to perform operations on multiple data elements simultaneously. SIMD is commonly used for optimizing performance in various domains, including multimedia processing, scientific computing, and data analysis. Below are the steps to program with SIMD:

Understand SIMD Architecture:

- Get acquainted with the SIMD architecture of the target processor. Common SIMD instruction sets include SSE (Streaming SIMD Extensions) on x86, NEON on ARM, and AVX (Advanced Vector Extensions) on modern x86-64 CPUs.

Choose a Programming Language:

- SIMD programming can be done in low-level assembly, but it's more common to use higher-level languages with SIMD support. C and C++ are popular choices due to their close-to-the-metal capabilities.

Select a Compiler/Toolchain:

- Use a compiler that supports SIMD instructions. Popular choices include GCC and Clang for C/C++, or MSVC for Windows development.

Enable SIMD Compiler Flags:

- Configure your compiler to use SIMD instructions. This may involve specifying compiler flags or options like -mavx for AVX support or -msse for SSE support.

Vectorize Your Code:

- Identify performance-critical parts of your code where SIMD optimization can be applied.

- Modify your code to use SIMD-enabled data types and operations. In C/C++, you can use data types like __m128 (SSE) or __m256 (AVX) for representing SIMD vectors.
- Replace scalar operations with SIMD operations that can process multiple data elements at once.

Use SIMD Intrinsics:

- Employ SIMD intrinsics provided by your compiler to directly call SIMD instructions. Intrinsics are platform-specific functions that map directly to assembly instructions.
- Example for adding two vectors using SSE intrinsics:

```
#include <immintrin.h> //
Include SIMD intrinsics header
```

```c
void add_vectors(float* a,
float* b, float* result, int
length) {
    int i;
    for (i = 0; i < length; i +=
4) {
        __m128 va =
_mm_load_ps(&a[i]); // Load four
floats from a
        __m128 vb =
_mm_load_ps(&b[i]); // Load four
floats from b
        __m128 vr =
_mm_add_ps(va, vb); // Add the
vectors
        _mm_store_ps(&result[i],
vr);    // Store the result
    }
}
```

Optimize Data Layout:

- Pay attention to data layout and memory access patterns to maximize SIMD performance.

Cache-friendly data structures
and aligned memory accesses
are crucial.

Compile and Test:

- Compile your code with the appropriate compiler flags.
- Test your program thoroughly to ensure correctness and measure performance improvements.

Profile and Optimize:

- Use profiling tools to identify performance bottlenecks in your code.
- Optimize your SIMD code further by applying loop unrolling, loop vectorization, and other optimization techniques.

Keep Portability in Mind:

- Be aware that SIMD code can be highly platform-specific. Consider providing fallback implementations for platforms that do not support SIMD

instructions to maintain
portability.

Document Your Code:

- Document your SIMD
  optimizations and intrinsics
  usage for better maintainability.

Stay Up-to-Date:

- SIMD instruction sets evolve, so
  stay updated with the latest
  SIMD extensions and
  capabilities offered by modern
  processors.

SIMD programming can significantly boost performance in various applications, but it requires careful consideration of hardware-specific details and a strong understanding of the target platform's SIMD architecture. While SIMD programming can be challenging, it's a powerful tool for achieving high performance in computational tasks.

Creating a simple SIMD program

Creating a simple SIMD (Single Instruction, Multiple Data) program can be a bit complex due to platform-specific differences and compiler support. In this example, I'll provide a basic SIMD program in C/C++ using SSE (Streaming SIMD Extensions) intrinsics to add two arrays of single-precision floating-point numbers element-wise. SSE is a common SIMD instruction set available on x86 architecture. Please note that the exact intrinsics may vary depending on your compiler and platform.

Here's a simple SIMD program:

```cpp
#include <iostream>
#include <immintrin.h> // Include SSE intrinsics

int main() {
    const int num_elements = 16; // Number of elements in each array
```

```cpp
    // Define two arrays of
single-precision floating-point
numbers
    float array1[num_elements];
    float array2[num_elements];

    // Initialize the arrays
with sample data
    for (int i = 0; i <
num_elements; ++i) {
        array1[i] =
static_cast<float>(i);
        array2[i] =
static_cast<float>(2 * i);
    }

    // Create arrays to store
the result
    float result[num_elements];

    // SIMD addition using SSE
intrinsics
    __m128 xmm1, xmm2,
xmm_result;
```

```cpp
    for (int i = 0; i <
num_elements; i += 4) {
        // Load four floats from
each array into xmm registers
        xmm1 =
_mm_load_ps(&array1[i]);
        xmm2 =
_mm_load_ps(&array2[i]);

        // Perform SIMD addition
        xmm_result =
_mm_add_ps(xmm1, xmm2);

        // Store the result in
the result array
        _mm_store_ps(&result[i],
xmm_result);
    }

    // Display the result
    std::cout << "Result: ";
    for (int i = 0; i <
num_elements; ++i) {
```

```cpp
        std::cout << result[i]
<< " ";
    }
    std::cout << std::endl;

    return 0;
}
```

Here's how this simple SIMD program
works:

- We define two arrays array1 and
  array2 of single-precision
  floating-point numbers and initialize
  them with sample data.
- We create an array result to store the
  SIMD addition result.
- Inside the loop, we use SSE intrinsics
  to load four floats from each of array1
  and array2 into SSE registers (xmm1
  and xmm2), perform the SIMD
  addition, and store the result back in
  the result array.
- Finally, we display the result.

To compile and run this program:

Ensure you have a C++ compiler that supports SSE intrinsics (most modern compilers do).

Save the code above to a .cpp file (e.g., simd_addition.cpp).

Compile the program:

```
g++ -o simd_program simd_addition.cpp -msse
```

This command compiles the program and specifies the -msse flag to enable SSE instructions.

Run the program:

```
./simd_program
```

You should see the result, which is the element-wise sum of the two arrays. This program demonstrates a basic use of SIMD intrinsics for parallel computation using SSE. Note that SIMD programming can be highly platform-specific, so the exact intrinsics may vary based on your compiler and target architecture.

How to program with C++

Programming with C++ involves writing code in the C++ programming language. C++ is a versatile language known for its performance, flexibility, and wide range of applications, including software development, game development, system programming, and more. Here are the steps to program with C++:

Set Up a Development Environment:

- Install a C++ development environment or Integrated Development Environment (IDE) on your computer. Popular choices include Visual Studio (for Windows), Xcode (for macOS), Code::Blocks, CLion, and Visual Studio Code (cross-platform).

Learn the Basics of C++:

- Familiarize yourself with C++ syntax and fundamental concepts, including variables, data types, operators, control structures (if statements, loops), functions, and classes.

Choose a Text Editor or IDE:

- Select a text editor or integrated development environment (IDE) suitable for C++ development. IDEs often provide features like code highlighting, debugging, and project management.

Write C++ Code:

- Create a new C++ source code file with a .cpp extension using your chosen text editor or IDE.
- Write C++ code to solve a specific problem or implement a program. Start with simple examples to grasp the language's syntax.

Compile the C++ Code:

- Compile your C++ code into an executable file using a C++ compiler. The compiler translates your human-readable code into machine-executable code.

- For example, using the GNU Compiler Collection (g++):

```
g++ -o my_program my_program.cpp
```

- This command compiles my_program.cpp and produces an executable named my_program.

Run the Program:

- Execute the compiled program:

```
./my_program
```

-
- Your program's output (if any) will be displayed in the terminal.

Debug and Test:

- Debug your program to find and fix errors or unexpected behavior. Most IDEs provide debugging tools.
- Write test cases to verify that your program behaves as expected.

Learn More Advanced C++ Features:

- Explore advanced C++ features such as object-oriented programming (classes and inheritance), templates, exceptions, and the Standard Template Library (STL) for data structures and algorithms.

Version Control:

- Use version control systems like Git to manage your code, track changes, and collaborate with others.

Document Your Code:

- Write comments and documentation to make your code more understandable and maintainable. Proper documentation is essential when working on larger projects.

Explore C++ Libraries and Frameworks:

- C++ has a vast ecosystem of libraries and frameworks for

various purposes. Familiarize yourself with relevant libraries to simplify complex tasks.

Practice and Build Projects:

- The best way to become proficient in C++ is through practice. Work on projects, solve coding challenges, and collaborate with others.

Follow Best Practices:

- Adhere to best practices in C++ programming, such as using descriptive variable names, following naming conventions, and writing efficient code.

Learn C++ Standards:

- Stay up-to-date with C++ standards (e.g., C++11, C++14, C++17, C++20), as they introduce new language features and improvements.

Programming with C++ offers a wide range of opportunities, whether you are interested in application development, game development, systems programming, or embedded programming. It's a versatile language with a strong community and extensive resources for learning and development.

Creating a simple C++ program

Let's create a simple C++ program that calculates the sum of two numbers entered by the user. This program will illustrate basic input/output operations and arithmetic calculations in C++.

```cpp
#include <iostream> // Include
the standard input/output
library

int main() {
    // Declare variables to
store the user's input and the
result
        double num1, num2, sum;
```

```cpp
    // Prompt the user to enter
the first number
    std::cout << "Enter the
first number: ";
    std::cin >> num1; // Read
the user's input

    // Prompt the user to enter
the second number
    std::cout << "Enter the
second number: ";
    std::cin >> num2; // Read
the user's input

    // Calculate the sum
    sum = num1 + num2;

    // Display the result
    std::cout << "The sum is: "
<< sum << std::endl;

    return 0; // Return 0 to
indicate successful program
execution
```

}

Here's how this simple C++ program works:
- We include the iostream header to use input and output functions.
- Inside the main function:
  - We declare three variables: num1, num2, and sum to store the user's input and the result of the addition.
  - We use std::cout to display a prompt to the user, asking them to enter the first number.
  - We use std::cin to read the user's input and store it in the num1 variable.
  - We repeat the process to get the second number from the user and store it in the num2 variable.
  - We calculate the sum of num1 and num2 and store it in the sum variable.

- Finally, we use std::cout to display the result to the user.
- The program then returns 0 to indicate successful execution.

To compile and run this C++ program:

Save the code above to a .cpp file (e.g., sum.cpp).

Open your terminal or command prompt.

Navigate to the directory where you saved the .cpp file.

Compile the program using a C++ compiler (e.g., g++):

```
g++ -o sum_program sum.cpp
```

Run the program:

```
./sum_program
```

You'll be prompted to enter two numbers, and the program will display their sum. This simple program demonstrates the basics of C++ input/output and variable usage. C++ offers a wide range of features for building more complex and powerful applications.

How to program with C

Programming with C involves writing code in the C programming language, a widely used and versatile language known for its simplicity and performance. C is commonly used for system programming, embedded systems, and developing low-level software. Here's how to get started with programming in C:

Set Up a Development Environment:

- Install a C compiler on your computer. Popular choices include GCC (GNU Compiler Collection), Clang, and Microsoft Visual C/C++.

Choose a Text Editor or IDE:

- Select a text editor or Integrated Development Environment (IDE) suitable for C programming. IDEs often provide features like code highlighting, debugging, and project management.

Learn the Basics of C:

- Start by understanding C syntax and fundamental concepts. Learn about variables, data types, operators, control structures (if statements, loops), functions, and basic I/O operations.

Write C Code:

- Create a new C source code file with a .c extension using your chosen text editor or IDE.
- Write C code to solve a specific problem or implement a program. Begin with simple examples to grasp the language's syntax.

Compile the C Code:

- Compile your C code into an executable file using a C compiler. The compiler translates your human-readable code into machine-executable code.

- For example, using GCC:

```
gcc -o my_program my_program.c
```

  - This command compiles my_program.c and produces an executable named my_program.

Run the Program:

- Execute the compiled program:

```
./my_program
```

  -

  - Your program's output (if any) will be displayed in the terminal.

Debug and Test:

- Debug your program to find and fix errors or unexpected behavior. Most IDEs provide debugging tools.
- Write test cases to verify that your program behaves as expected.

Learn More Advanced C Features:

- Explore advanced C features such as pointers, memory

management, structures, unions, file I/O, and libraries like the C Standard Library.

Version Control:

- Use version control systems like Git to manage your code, track changes, and collaborate with others.

Document Your Code:

- Write comments and documentation to make your code more understandable and maintainable. Proper documentation is essential when working on larger projects.

Explore C Libraries and Frameworks:

- C has a vast ecosystem of libraries and frameworks for various purposes. Familiarize yourself with relevant libraries to simplify complex tasks.

Practice and Build Projects:

- The best way to become proficient in C is through

practice. Work on projects, solve coding challenges, and collaborate with others.

Follow Best Practices:

- Adhere to best practices in C programming, such as using descriptive variable names, following naming conventions, and writing efficient code.

Stay Up-to-Date:

- Keep yourself updated with the latest developments in the C programming language, including updates to the C standard.

Programming in C offers a robust foundation for system-level and low-level software development. It's a versatile language that can be used in various domains, including operating systems, device drivers, embedded systems, and more.

Creating a simple C program

Let's create a simple C program that calculates the sum of two numbers entered by the user. This program will demonstrate basic input/output operations and arithmetic calculations in C.

```c
#include <stdio.h> // Include
the standard input/output
library


int main() {
    // Declare variables to
store the user's input and the
result
    double num1, num2, sum;

    // Prompt the user to enter
the first number
    printf("Enter the first
number: ");
    scanf("%lf", &num1); // Read
the user's input
```

```c
    // Prompt the user to enter
the second number
    printf("Enter the second
number: ");
    scanf("%lf", &num2); // Read
the user's input

    // Calculate the sum
    sum = num1 + num2;

    // Display the result
    printf("The sum is: %lf\n",
sum);

    return 0; // Return 0 to
indicate successful program
execution
}
```

Here's how this simple C program works:
- We include the stdio.h header to use
  input and output functions.
- Inside the main function:

- We declare three variables: num1, num2, and sum to store the user's input and the result of the addition.
- We use printf to display a prompt to the user, asking them to enter the first number.
- We use scanf to read the user's input as a double-precision floating-point number (%lf) and store it in the num1 variable.
- We repeat the process to get the second number from the user and store it in the num2 variable.
- We calculate the sum of num1 and num2 and store it in the sum variable.
- Finally, we use printf to display the result to the user.
- The program then returns 0 to indicate successful execution.

To compile and run this C program:

Save the code above to a .c file (e.g., sum.c).
Open your terminal or command prompt.
Navigate to the directory where you saved the .c file.
Compile the program using a C compiler (e.g., gcc):

```
gcc -o sum_program sum.c
```

Run the program:

```
./sum_program
```

You'll be prompted to enter two numbers, and the program will display their sum. This simple program demonstrates the basics of C input/output and variable usage. C is a foundational language used for system-level and low-level programming, making it a valuable skill for various software development tasks.

Scripting languages play a vital role in modern software development and automation. Their importance stems from several key advantages and use cases:

Ease of Learning and Use:

- Scripting languages are typically easy to learn and use, making them accessible to both beginners and experienced programmers. They often have concise and human-readable syntax, which simplifies code development and debugging.

Rapid Development:

- Scripting languages are well-suited for rapid application development (RAD). Developers can quickly write, test, and iterate on scripts, which accelerates the software development lifecycle.

Scripting Automation:

- Scripting languages are frequently used for automating repetitive tasks and processes. This includes automating system administration, file manipulation, data processing, and more. Scripting can save time and reduce human error in these tasks.

Web Development:

- Many popular web technologies and frameworks, such as JavaScript, Python (with Django and Flask), Ruby (with Ruby on Rails), and PHP, are scripting languages. They are used to build dynamic and interactive websites and web applications.

Data Analysis and Visualization:

- Scripting languages like Python and R are extensively used in data analysis, scientific computing, and data visualization. Libraries and frameworks like NumPy, pandas, and Matplotlib make data manipulation and visualization accessible.

Prototyping:

- Scripting languages are often used for creating prototypes and proof-of-concept applications. Their rapid development capabilities make it easier to experiment with new ideas and concepts before committing to full-scale development.

Cross-Platform Compatibility:

- Many scripting languages are platform-independent, meaning scripts can run on various operating systems without modification. This cross-platform compatibility enhances the portability of applications and scripts.

Extensibility and Integration:

- Scripting languages can be embedded within other applications to provide extensibility. For example, Python can be embedded in

C/C++ applications, allowing developers to create custom scripting capabilities.

Automation of System Administration:

- Scripting languages are indispensable for automating system administration tasks. Shell scripts in Unix-like systems (e.g., Bash) and PowerShell scripts in Windows are examples of how scripting languages simplify administrative tasks.

Prototyping:

- Scripting languages are often used for creating prototypes and proof-of-concept applications. Their rapid development capabilities make it easier to experiment with new ideas and concepts before committing to full-scale development.

IoT and Embedded Systems:

- Scripting languages like Python and Lua are used in Internet of Things (IoT) and embedded systems development due to their small footprint and ability to interact with hardware.

Web Scraping and Data Extraction:

- Scripting languages are popular choices for web scraping and data extraction tasks. Developers can write scripts to crawl websites and extract information for analysis or storage.

Testing and Automation Frameworks:

- Many testing frameworks, automation tools, and continuous integration/continuous deployment (CI/CD) pipelines use scripting languages to define and execute test cases and automated workflows.

Game Development:

- Some scripting languages like Lua are used for game development to define game logic and behavior. Game engines often provide scripting support for customization.

Education and Learning:

- Scripting languages are commonly used for teaching programming concepts due to their simplicity and immediate feedback. They serve as excellent educational tools for students and beginners.

Overall, scripting languages offer a versatile and practical solution for a wide range of tasks, from simple automation to complex software development. Their ease of use, rapid development capabilities, and broad applicability make them a crucial part of the software development landscape.

Example of Scripting Languages and their specific functions

Here are some examples of scripting languages and their specific functions:

Python:

- Web Development: Python is used for building web applications and websites with frameworks like Django and Flask.
- Data Analysis: Python, along with libraries like pandas and NumPy, is widely used for data manipulation and analysis.
- Automation: Python scripts can automate various tasks, from file management to data extraction.
- Machine Learning and AI: Python is the language of choice for developing machine learning models using libraries like TensorFlow and scikit-learn.

JavaScript:

- Web Development: JavaScript is primarily used for building dynamic and interactive web applications. It's a client-side scripting language.

- Web Browser Manipulation: JavaScript can manipulate and interact with elements on web pages, enabling features like form validation and dynamic content loading.
- Server-Side Development: Node.js allows JavaScript to be used for server-side development as well.

Ruby:

- Web Development: Ruby is known for its web development framework, Ruby on Rails, which simplifies the creation of web applications.
- Automation: Ruby scripts can automate various tasks, making it a handy scripting language for system administrators.

- Testing: Ruby is used for testing frameworks like RSpec and Cucumber.

Perl:

- Text Processing: Perl excels at text processing, making it ideal for parsing and manipulating large data sets and log files.
- Scripting: Perl is often used for system administration, automation, and creating scripts for various tasks.
- Regular Expressions: Perl has powerful regular expression capabilities, making it valuable for pattern matching and extraction.

Bash:

- Shell Scripting: Bash (Bourne Again Shell) is the default shell on many Unix-like operating systems and is used for system administration, automation, and creating shell scripts.

- Command Line Operations: It's used for executing command line operations and managing processes on Linux and macOS.

PHP:

- Web Development: PHP is a server-side scripting language used for building dynamic web applications and websites.
- Database Interaction: PHP is often used to interact with databases, such as MySQL, to retrieve and manipulate data.

Lua:

- Game Development: Lua is commonly used as a scripting language for game engines like Unity and Unreal Engine, where it defines game logic and behavior.
- Embedding: Lua is often embedded in other applications to provide scripting capabilities.

PowerShell:

- Windows Automation:
  PowerShell is a Windows-centric
  scripting language used for
  system administration, task
  automation, and managing
  Windows-based systems.
- Azure Cloud Automation:
  PowerShell is widely used for
  automating tasks and managing
  resources in Microsoft Azure
  cloud environments.

Tcl (Tool Command Language):
- Scripting and Automation: Tcl is
  known for its use in automation
  and scripting, particularly in the
  context of network devices and
  embedded systems.
- GUI Development: Tcl/Tk is
  used for creating graphical user
  interfaces (GUIs).

Awk:
- Text Processing: Awk is a
  versatile language for text

processing and data extraction from structured text files.

- Report Generation: It is often used to generate custom reports based on text data.

These are just a few examples of scripting languages and their primary functions. Each language has its strengths and weaknesses, making them suitable for specific tasks and domains. Depending on the requirements of a particular project, developers may choose the scripting language that best fits their needs.

How to program with PHP

Programming with PHP involves creating web applications and dynamic websites using the PHP scripting language. PHP is a server-side scripting language commonly used for web development. Here are the steps to get started with programming in PHP:

Set Up a Development Environment:

- Install a web server (e.g., Apache, Nginx) and PHP on your computer. Alternatively, use a pre-packaged web development environment like XAMPP or WAMP that includes Apache, PHP, and MySQL.

Choose a Text Editor or IDE:

- Select a text editor or Integrated Development Environment (IDE) suitable for PHP development. Popular choices include Visual Studio Code, PhpStorm, and NetBeans.

Create a PHP File:

- Create a new file with a .php extension. This will be your PHP script.

Write PHP Code:

- Write PHP code within the PHP tags (<?php and ?>). This is where you'll put your PHP logic.

- Here's an example of a simple PHP script that displays "Hello, World!":

```php
<?php
echo "Hello, World!";
?>
```

-

Start a Local Web Server:
  - If you're not using a pre-packaged environment, start your local web server (e.g., Apache) to serve PHP files.
  - Verify that PHP is working by creating a PHP info file (info.php) with the following content and accessing it in your web browser:

```php
<?php
phpinfo();
?>
```

-

Access PHP Files:

- Place your PHP files in the web server's document root or public directory.
- Access your PHP files through a web browser by navigating to http://localhost/your-file.php.

Learn PHP Basics:

- Familiarize yourself with the basics of PHP, including variables, data types, operators, control structures (if statements, loops), functions, and arrays. The PHP documentation is a valuable resource for learning.

Database Interaction:

- Learn how to interact with databases using PHP. MySQL and MariaDB are commonly used databases with PHP. Utilize PHP's database functions (e.g., mysqli or PDO) to perform database operations.

Forms and User Input:

- Understand how to handle form submissions and user input using PHP. Validate and process data sent from HTML forms.

Error Handling:

- Learn about PHP error handling techniques, including error reporting, exception handling, and debugging tools.

Include External Files:

- PHP allows you to include external files, which can help organize and modularize your code.

Security:

- Study PHP security best practices to prevent common vulnerabilities like SQL injection and cross-site scripting (XSS).

Session Management and Cookies:

- Learn how to manage user sessions and use cookies to maintain user state.

File Handling:

- Understand file handling in PHP, including reading and writing files, uploading files, and directory manipulation.

Learn About Frameworks:

- Explore PHP frameworks like Laravel, Symfony, and CodeIgniter to streamline web development and follow best practices.

Testing and Deployment:

- Test your PHP applications thoroughly and prepare for deployment on a production server.

Documentation:

- Document your PHP code using comments and follow coding standards to enhance maintainability.

Practice and Build Projects:

- The best way to become proficient in PHP is through practice. Work on real projects, build web applications, and experiment with various features and libraries.

PHP is a versatile scripting language widely used for web development, so mastering it opens up opportunities to create dynamic and interactive web applications.

Creating a simple PHP program

Let's create a simple PHP program that displays "Hello, World!" in a web browser. This example will demonstrate the basic structure of a PHP script and how to run it locally on a web server. Here are the steps:

Set Up a Development Environment:

- Make sure you have a web server with PHP support installed. If you don't have one, consider using a package like XAMPP, which includes Apache, PHP, and MySQL bundled together.

Create a PHP File:

- Open your text editor and create a new file named hello.php.

Write PHP Code:

- Inside hello.php, write the following PHP code:

```php
<!DOCTYPE html>
<html>
<head>
    <title>Hello, World!</title>
</head>
<body>
    <h1><?php echo "Hello,
World!"; ?></h1>
</body>
</html>
```

In this code:

- We embed PHP code within `<?php` and `?>` tags.
- Inside the HTML body, we use `<?php echo "Hello, World!"; ?>` to display "Hello, World!" within an `<h1>` heading.

Save the PHP File:

- Save the hello.php file in the web server's document root directory. In XAMPP, this directory is typically htdocs within the XAMPP installation directory.

Start the Web Server:

- If you're using XAMPP, start the Apache web server from the XAMPP control panel.

Access the PHP Script:

- Open your web browser and enter the following URL:

http://localhost/hello.php

- You should see a web page displaying "Hello, World!" as an <h1> heading.

This simple PHP program demonstrates the basics of embedding PHP code within an HTML document. You can build more complex web applications by adding PHP logic for handling user input, connecting to databases, and creating dynamic content. PHP is widely used in web development for building dynamic websites and web applications.

How to program with Perl

Programming with Perl involves writing scripts and programs using the Perl programming language. Perl is known for its text-processing capabilities and is commonly used for tasks like data manipulation, report generation, and system administration. Here's how to get started with programming in Perl:

Install Perl:

- If Perl is not already installed on your system, download and install it from the official Perl website (https://www.perl.org/get.html) or use the package manager for your operating system (e.g., apt-get for Linux or ActivePerl for Windows).

Choose a Text Editor:

- Select a text editor or Integrated Development Environment (IDE) suitable for Perl development. Popular choices include Visual Studio Code, Perl-specific editors like Padre, and general-purpose editors like Notepad++.

Create a Perl Script:

- Create a new file with a .pl extension. This will be your Perl script.
- You can create a Perl script using any text editor.

Write Perl Code:

- Inside your Perl script, write Perl code. Perl uses straightforward syntax for text processing and scripting tasks.
- Here's an example of a simple Perl script that prints "Hello, Perl!" to the console:

```perl
#!/usr/bin/perl
use strict;
```

```perl
use warnings;

print "Hello, Perl!\n";
```

- In this example:
    - #!/usr/bin/perl is called a shebang line and indicates the path to the Perl interpreter.
    - use strict; and use warnings; are pragmas that help enforce good coding practices and catch potential issues.

Run the Perl Script:

- Open your terminal or command prompt.
- Navigate to the directory where you saved your Perl script.
- Run the Perl script using the Perl interpreter:

```
perl scriptname.pl
```

- Replace scriptname.pl with the name of your Perl script.

Learn Perl Basics:

- Familiarize yourself with Perl's basic features, including variables, data types, operators, control structures (if statements, loops), functions, and regular expressions.
- Explore Perl's extensive standard library and modules for various tasks.

Text Processing:

- Perl is renowned for its text processing capabilities. Learn about Perl's regular expression support and string manipulation functions for effective text processing.

File I/O:

- Understand how to read and write files using Perl. You can work with text files, CSV files, and more.

Modules and Libraries:

- Perl has a vast ecosystem of
  modules and libraries available
  on CPAN (Comprehensive Perl
  Archive Network). Learn how to
  use and install Perl modules to
  extend the language's
  functionality.

Error Handling:

- Learn about error handling
  techniques in Perl, including the
  use of die and warn functions.

Practice and Build Projects:

- The best way to become
  proficient in Perl is through
  practice. Work on projects,
  create scripts for automation,
  and solve real-world tasks using
  Perl.

Documentation:

- Document your Perl code using
  comments and follow Perl
  coding conventions to improve
  code maintainability.

Testing:

- Consider writing test scripts using Perl's testing framework (e.g., Test::Simple) to ensure your code behaves as expected.

Perl's power lies in its ability to handle text processing tasks efficiently. While it's commonly used for scripting and system administration, it can also be used for web development, automation, and a wide range of other applications.

Creating a simple Perl program

Let's create a simple Perl program that prompts the user for their name and then greets them. This program will demonstrate basic input/output operations in Perl.

Create a Perl Script:

Open a text editor and create a new file with a .pl extension. For example, name it greet.pl.

Write Perl Code:

Inside greet.pl, write the following Perl code:

```perl
#!/usr/bin/perl
use strict;
use warnings;

# Prompt the user for their name
print "Enter your name: ";
my $name = <STDIN>; # Read user
input from the standard input

# Remove newline character from
the input
chomp $name;

# Greet the user
print "Hello, $name! Welcome to
Perl!\n";
```

In this code:

- #!/usr/bin/perl is the shebang line that specifies the path to the Perl interpreter.
- use strict; and use warnings; are pragmas that enforce good coding practices and catch potential issues.

- We use print to display a prompt and ask the user to enter their name.
- We use <STDIN> to read the user's input from the standard input (keyboard).
- chomp $name; removes the newline character from the input to ensure a clean display.
- Finally, we use print to greet the user by displaying their name.

Run the Perl Script:

Open your terminal or command prompt.

Navigate to the directory where you saved your Perl script (greet.pl).

Run the Perl script using the Perl interpreter:

```
perl greet.pl
```

You will be prompted to enter your name. After entering your name, the program will greet you. For example:

```
Enter your name: John
Hello, John! Welcome to Perl!
```

This simple Perl program demonstrates how to prompt the user for input, process the input, and display output. Perl is often used for tasks involving text processing and automation, making it a versatile scripting language.

How to program with Awk

Programming with Awk involves writing scripts and programs using the Awk scripting language. Awk is a versatile language primarily used for text processing and manipulation. Here's how to get started with programming in Awk:

Open a Terminal or Command Prompt:

- To begin programming in Awk, open a terminal or command prompt on your computer.

Create an Awk Script:

- Awk programs are typically written as one-liners or saved in a text file with a .awk extension. For this example, let's create a simple one-liner Awk script.

Write Awk Code:

- In the terminal or command prompt, you can use the awk command to write and execute one-liner scripts. Here's an example of a basic Awk script that prints "Hello, Awk!" to the console:

```
echo "Hello, World!" | awk '{ print "Hello, Awk!" }'
```

- In this example, the echo command outputs "Hello, World!" to the standard input (| pipes the output to the awk command). The awk script in single quotes ('...') consists of a single action that prints "Hello, Awk!".

Run the Awk Script:

- After writing your Awk script in the terminal, press Enter to execute it. You should see the output:

```
Hello, Awk!
```

-

Learn Awk Basics:
- Familiarize yourself with the basic features of Awk, including patterns, actions, and variables.
- Understand how to use built-in variables like $0 (the entire input line) and $1, $2, etc. (field variables).

Text Processing:
- Awk is renowned for its text processing capabilities. Learn how to use regular expressions, field separators, and various built-in functions for manipulating text data.

File I/O:
- Explore how to read and write files using Awk. Awk can process files line by line or perform complex data transformations.

Awk Script Files:

- Instead of one-liners, you can save your Awk scripts in .awk files and execute them using the awk command. Create a file, e.g., myscript.awk, and write your Awk code in it.

```
# This is a comment
BEGIN {
    print "Hello from Awk
Script!"
}
```

- Execute the script using:

```
awk -f myscript.awk
```

Practice and Build Projects:

- Practice using Awk to solve real-world text-processing tasks. Create scripts for data extraction, report generation, and more.

Documentation:

- Refer to the Awk documentation and manuals to deepen your

understanding of the language's capabilities.

Community and Resources:

- Explore online resources, forums, and books related to Awk programming to enhance your skills.

Awk is an efficient and expressive language for text processing and manipulation. It's often used in conjunction with other Unix tools to perform complex data transformations and analysis. Learning Awk can significantly improve your ability to work with structured text data.

Creating a simple Awk program

Let's create a simple Awk program that reads a CSV (Comma-Separated Values) file, extracts specific columns, and calculates the sum of values in one of those columns. This example will demonstrate the basic syntax and features of Awk for text processing.

Assume you have a CSV file named data.csv with the following content:

```
Name,Age,Salary
John,30,50000
Alice,28,48000
Bob,35,60000
Eva,32,55000
```

Now, create an Awk script to read this CSV file and calculate the sum of salaries:

```
      Open a Text Editor:
      Open a text editor, such as
      awk_script.awk, to write
      your Awk program.
      Write Awk Code:
      Inside awk_script.awk, write
      the following Awk code:
#!/usr/bin/awk -f

BEGIN {
    FS = ","  # Set the field
separator to a comma (CSV)
```

```awk
    total_salary = 0   # Initialize the total_salary variable
}

# Process each line of the CSV file
{
    name = $1
    age = $2
    salary = $3

    # Print the name and salary
    print "Name:", name, " Salary:", salary

    # Add the salary to the total
    total_salary += salary
}

# After processing all lines, print the total salary
END {
```

```
    print "Total Salary:",
total_salary
}
```

In this code:

- #!/usr/bin/awk -f is the shebang line that specifies the path to the Awk interpreter and the -f option to read the script from a file.
- BEGIN is a special block that runs before processing any lines. We set the field separator (FS) to a comma and initialize total_salary to zero.
- The main block processes each line of the CSV file:
    - We assign the values of each field (Name, Age, Salary) to variables (name, age, salary).
    - We print the Name and Salary for each person.
    - We add the salary to total_salary.

- END is another special block that runs after processing all lines. We print the total salary.

Run the Awk Script:

Open your terminal or command prompt.

Navigate to the directory where you saved your Awk script (awk_script.awk).

Run the Awk script using the Awk interpreter:

```
awk -f awk_script.awk data.csv
```

Replace data.csv with the path to your CSV file if it's not in the same directory.

View the Output:

You will see the program's output, which includes the name and salary of each person in the CSV file and the total salary:

```
Name: John   Salary: 50000
Name: Alice   Salary: 48000
Name: Bob   Salary: 60000
Name: Eva   Salary: 55000
```

```
Total Salary: 213000
```

This simple Awk program demonstrates how to process text files, split lines into fields, perform calculations, and generate reports. Awk is a powerful tool for text manipulation and is commonly used for data processing in Unix-like environments.

How to program with Tcl

Programming with Tcl (Tool Command Language) involves writing scripts and programs using the Tcl scripting language. Tcl is known for its simplicity and is commonly used for a wide range of tasks, including automation, creating graphical user interfaces (GUIs), and embedded scripting. Here's how to get started with programming in Tcl:

Install Tcl:

- If Tcl is not already installed on your system, download and install it from the official Tcl

website
(https://www.tcl.tk/download.html) or use your operating system's package manager.

Choose a Text Editor or IDE:

- Select a text editor or Integrated Development Environment (IDE) suitable for Tcl development. Popular choices include Visual Studio Code, ActiveTcl, and Tcl Dev Kit.

Create a Tcl Script:

- Create a new file with a .tcl extension. This will be your Tcl script.
- You can create a Tcl script using any text editor.

Write Tcl Code:

- Inside your Tcl script, write Tcl code. Tcl has a simple syntax characterized by commands and arguments. Here's an example of a basic Tcl script that prints "Hello, Tcl!" to the console:

```tcl
# This is a comment
puts "Hello, Tcl!"
```

- In this code:
  - # This is a comment is a comment line. Comments are preceded by a # character and are ignored by the Tcl interpreter.
  - puts is a command that prints text to the standard output.

Run the Tcl Script:

- Open your terminal or command prompt.
- Navigate to the directory where you saved your Tcl script.
- Run the Tcl script using the tclsh interpreter:

```
tclsh scriptname.tcl
```

- Replace scriptname.tcl with the name of your Tcl script.

Learn Tcl Basics:

- Familiarize yourself with the basic features of Tcl, including variables, control structures (if statements, loops), procedures (functions), and built-in commands.

Working with Tk (Tcl/Tk):

- If you intend to create graphical user interfaces (GUIs) with Tcl, you'll work with the Tk toolkit. Learn how to use Tk for creating windows, buttons, menus, and other GUI components.

Error Handling:

- Understand how to handle errors and exceptions in Tcl, including using the catch command.

File I/O:

- Learn how to read and write files using Tcl. Tcl provides file manipulation commands to work with text and binary files.

Tcl Modules and Packages:

- Explore Tcl modules and packages for extending Tcl's

functionality. The Tcl
community provides many
packages for various purposes.
Practice and Build Projects:

- Practice using Tcl to automate
  tasks, create scripts for system
  administration, and build small
  projects.

Documentation and Community:

- Refer to the Tcl documentation
  and manuals for in-depth
  knowledge and search for
  resources in the Tcl community
  to enhance your Tcl
  programming skills.

Tcl's simplicity and versatility make it a
suitable choice for various scripting and
automation tasks. Whether you're working
on system administration, creating GUI
applications, or embedding scripting
capabilities in other software, Tcl offers a
straightforward and powerful scripting
solution.

Creating a simple Tcl program

Let's create a simple Tcl program that prompts the user for their name and then greets them. This program will demonstrate basic input/output operations in Tcl.

Create a Tcl Script:
Open a text editor and create a new file with a .tcl extension. For example, name it greet.tcl.
Write Tcl Code:
Inside greet.tcl, write the following Tcl code:

```tcl
# Prompt the user for their name
puts "Enter your name: "
flush stdout

# Read user input
set name [gets stdin]

# Greet the user
puts "Hello, $name! Welcome to Tcl!"
```

In this code:

- # is used to add comments in Tcl. Comments are ignored by the interpreter and are for documentation purposes.
- puts is used to display the prompt and text to the standard output.
- flush stdout ensures that the text is immediately displayed in the console.
- set name [gets stdin] reads a line of input from the user and stores it in the variable name.
- Finally, we use puts again to greet the user by displaying their name.

Run the Tcl Script:

Open your terminal or command prompt.

Navigate to the directory where you saved your Tcl script (greet.tcl).

Run the Tcl script using the Tcl interpreter:

```
tclsh greet.tcl
```

Enter Your Name:
You will see the program's output,
which prompts you to enter your
name. For example:

```
Enter your name:
```

```
Type your name and press
Enter.
```

View the Output:
After entering your name, the
program will greet you. For example:

```
Hello, John! Welcome to Tcl!
```

This simple Tcl program demonstrates how
to prompt the user for input, read and store
the input, and display output. Tcl is known
for its simplicity and is often used for tasks
like automation, creating GUIs with Tk, and
embedding scripting capabilities in other
applications.

How to program with PowerShell

Programming with PowerShell involves writing scripts and programs using the PowerShell scripting language. PowerShell is primarily used for system administration, automation, and managing Windows-based systems. Here's how to get started with programming in PowerShell:

Open PowerShell:

- To begin programming in PowerShell, open a PowerShell console or Windows PowerShell ISE (Integrated Scripting Environment). PowerShell is pre-installed on most modern Windows operating systems.

Create a PowerShell Script:

- PowerShell scripts are typically written as .ps1 files. You can create a new script using any text editor or by using PowerShell ISE's script editor.

Write PowerShell Code:

- Inside your PowerShell script, write PowerShell code. PowerShell uses cmdlets (pronounced "command-lets") and scripting constructs to perform tasks. Here's an example of a basic PowerShell script that prints "Hello, PowerShell!" to the console:

```
# This is a comment
Write-Host "Hello, PowerShell!"
```

- In this code:
    - # This is a comment is a comment line. Comments are preceded by a # character and are ignored by the PowerShell interpreter.
    - Write-Host is a cmdlet used to display text in the console.

Run the PowerShell Script:

- Open your PowerShell console or ISE.

- Navigate to the directory where you saved your PowerShell script.
- Run the PowerShell script by entering its filename, including the .ps1 extension:

```
.\scriptname.ps1
```

- Replace scriptname.ps1 with the name of your PowerShell script.

Learn PowerShell Basics:

- Familiarize yourself with the basic features of PowerShell, including cmdlets, variables, data types, operators, control structures (if statements, loops), functions, and modules.

Working with Modules:

- PowerShell has a vast ecosystem of modules that extend its functionality. Learn how to use modules to add new cmdlets and capabilities to your scripts.

Error Handling:

- Understand how to handle errors and exceptions in PowerShell using the try, catch, and finally constructs.

Working with Objects:

- PowerShell is object-oriented, which means it deals with objects and properties. Learn how to work with objects, filter, and manipulate data.

File I/O:

- Learn how to read and write files using PowerShell. PowerShell provides cmdlets for working with files and directories.

Working with PowerShell Remoting:

- PowerShell Remoting allows you to execute PowerShell scripts on remote computers. Learn how to use PowerShell Remoting for remote administration.

Automation and Scripting:

- Explore automation tasks like scheduled jobs, task automation, and batch scripting.

Documentation and Help:

- PowerShell has extensive documentation and built-in help. Use the Get-Help cmdlet to access information about cmdlets and topics.

Practice and Build Projects:

- The best way to become proficient in PowerShell is through practice. Work on real-world system administration tasks, automate routine processes, and create custom scripts.

Community and Resources:

- Join the PowerShell community, participate in forums, and explore online resources and books related to PowerShell scripting.

PowerShell is a powerful scripting language for automating Windows-related tasks and managing systems. Whether you're an IT administrator or a developer, mastering PowerShell can greatly enhance your ability to work with Windows environments efficiently.

Creating a simple PowerShell program

Let's create a simple PowerShell program that prompts the user for their name and then greets them. This program will demonstrate basic input/output operations in PowerShell.

Open PowerShell:

Open a PowerShell console or Windows PowerShell ISE.

Create a PowerShell Script:

PowerShell scripts are typically written as .ps1 files. You can create a new script using a text editor or

PowerShell ISE's script editor. For this example, we'll use a text editor.
Write PowerShell Code:
Inside your text editor, write the following PowerShell code:

```
# Prompt the user for their name
Write-Host "Enter your name:"


# Read user input
$name = Read-Host


# Greet the user
Write-Host "Hello, $name!
Welcome to PowerShell!"
```

In this code:

- # is used for comments in PowerShell. Comments are ignored by the interpreter and are for documentation purposes.
- Write-Host is used to display the prompt and text to the console.
- $name = Read-Host reads user input and stores it in the variable $name.

- Finally, we use Write-Host again to greet the user by displaying their name.

Save the PowerShell Script:
Save the script with a .ps1 extension, such as greet.ps1. Make sure you save it in a location where you have write access.

Configure Execution Policy (If Needed):
PowerShell may have an execution policy that restricts running scripts. To check the current execution policy, open a PowerShell console and run:
powershell
If it's set to "Restricted," you may need to change it. To change the execution policy to allow local script execution (not recommended for production), run:

Set-ExecutionPolicy RemoteSigned
After running the script, you can set the execution policy back to a more secure setting if needed.

Run the PowerShell Script:
Open your PowerShell console.
Navigate to the directory where you saved your PowerShell script (greet.ps1).
Run the PowerShell script by entering its filename:

```
.\greet.ps1
```

PowerShell may ask if you want to run the script. Confirm by typing Y for Yes and pressing Enter.
Enter Your Name:
You will see the program's output, which prompts you to enter your name. For example:

```
Enter your name:
```

Type your name and press Enter.
View the Output:
After entering your name, the program will greet you. For example:

```
Hello, John! Welcome to PowerShell!
```

This simple PowerShell program demonstrates how to prompt the user for input, read and store the input, and display output. PowerShell is a versatile scripting language used for various tasks, including system administration, automation, and managing Windows-based systems.

How to program with Lua

Programming with Lua involves writing scripts and programs using the Lua programming language. Lua is a lightweight and embeddable scripting language known for its simplicity and efficiency. It's often used in game development, scripting for software applications, and embedded systems. Here's how to get started with programming in Lua:

Install Lua:

- If Lua is not already installed on your system, download and install it from the official Lua

website
(https://www.lua.org/download.html). You can choose from various distributions, including the standalone interpreter and libraries for embedding Lua in other applications.

Choose a Text Editor:

- Select a text editor or Integrated Development Environment (IDE) suitable for Lua development. Common choices include Visual Studio Code, Sublime Text, and dedicated Lua editors like ZeroBrane Studio.

Create a Lua Script:

- Lua scripts are typically saved with a .lua extension. Create a new file with this extension to start writing your Lua script.

Write Lua Code:

- Inside your Lua script, write Lua code. Lua has a straightforward syntax with minimalistic constructs. Here's an example of a basic Lua script that prints "Hello, Lua!" to the console:

```lua
-- This is a comment
print("Hello, Lua!")
```

- In this code:
    - -- is used to add comments in Lua. Comments are ignored by the interpreter and are for documentation purposes.
    - print("Hello, Lua!") is used to display text to the standard output.

Run the Lua Script:
- Open your terminal or command prompt.
- Navigate to the directory where you saved your Lua script.
- Run the Lua script using the Lua interpreter:

```
lua scriptname.lua
```

- Replace scriptname.lua with the name of your Lua script.

Learn Lua Basics:

- Familiarize yourself with the basic features of Lua, including variables, data types, operators, control structures (if statements, loops), functions, and tables (Lua's versatile data structure).

Error Handling:

- Understand how to handle errors and exceptions in Lua using pcall and assert.

Working with Tables:

- Lua's tables are versatile and serve various purposes, from arrays to dictionaries. Learn how to work with tables effectively.

Modules and Libraries:

- Explore Lua modules and libraries to extend Lua's functionality. LuaRocks (https://luarocks.org/) is a package manager for Lua that

makes it easy to install
third-party libraries.
Practice and Build Projects:

- The best way to become
  proficient in Lua is through
  practice. Work on projects,
  create scripts for games or
  applications, and explore Lua's
  use in embedding and
  extending.

Documentation and Community:

- Refer to the Lua documentation
  and manuals for detailed
  information about Lua's
  features. Join the Lua
  community, participate in
  forums, and explore online
  resources and books related to
  Lua programming.

Lua's simplicity and flexibility make it an
excellent choice for scripting and
embedding in a wide range of applications.
Whether you're working on game
development, automation, or scripting for

software applications, Lua offers a lightweight and efficient scripting solution.

Creating a simple Lua program

Let's create a simple Lua program that prompts the user for their name and then greets them. This program will demonstrate basic input/output operations in Lua.

Create a Lua Script:

Open a text editor and create a new file with a .lua extension. For example, name it greet.lua.

Write Lua Code:

Inside greet.lua, write the following Lua code:

```lua
-- Prompt the user for their name
io.write("Enter your name: ")
io.flush()

-- Read user input
local name = io.read()
```

```lua
-- Greet the user
print("Hello, " .. name .. "! Welcome to Lua!")
```

In this code:

- io.write("Enter your name: ") is used to display the prompt without a newline character.
- io.flush() ensures that the prompt is immediately displayed in the console.
- local name = io.read() reads a line of input from the user and stores it in the variable name.
- print("Hello, " .. name .. "! Welcome to Lua!") is used to greet the user by displaying their name.

Run the Lua Script:

Open your terminal or command prompt.

Navigate to the directory where you saved your Lua script (greet.lua).

Run the Lua script using the Lua interpreter:

```
lua greet.lua
```

Enter Your Name:
You will see the program's output,
which prompts you to enter your
name. For example:

```
Enter your name:
```

```
Type your name and press
Enter.
```

View the Output:
After entering your name, the
program will greet you. For example:

```
Hello, John! Welcome to Lua!
```

This simple Lua program demonstrates how
to prompt the user for input, read and store
the input, and display output. Lua's
straightforward syntax and flexibility make
it suitable for various scripting tasks and
embedding in applications.

How to program with Bash

Programming with Bash involves writing scripts and programs using the Bash (Bourne Again Shell) scripting language. Bash is commonly used in Unix-like operating systems for automation, system administration, and running command-line tasks. Here's how to get started with programming in Bash:

Open a Terminal:
To begin programming in Bash, open a terminal or command prompt on your Unix-like operating system. Bash is often the default shell on Linux and macOS.
Create a Bash Script:
Bash scripts are typically saved with a .sh extension. Create a new file with this extension to start writing your Bash script.
Write Bash Code:
Inside your Bash script, write Bash code. Bash scripts are a sequence of shell commands and control

structures. Here's an example of a basic Bash script that prints "Hello, Bash!" to the console:

```bash
#!/bin/bash
```

```bash
# This is a comment
echo "Hello, Bash!"
```

In this code:

- #!/bin/bash is called a shebang line and specifies the path to the Bash interpreter. It tells the system that this script should be executed with Bash.
- # is used for comments in Bash. Comments are ignored by the interpreter and are for documentation purposes.
- echo is used to display text to the standard output.

Make the Script Executable:

Before you can run the Bash script, you need to make it executable. In your terminal, navigate to the

directory where you saved your script
and run the following command:

```
chmod +x scriptname.sh
```

Replace scriptname.sh with the name
of your Bash script.
Run the Bash Script:
To run the Bash script, you can simply
type:

```
./scriptname.sh
```

Replace scriptname.sh with the name
of your script.
Learn Bash Basics:
Familiarize yourself with the basic
features of Bash, including variables,
command substitution, loops,
conditionals (if statements), functions,
and file manipulation.
Command-Line Arguments:
Understand how to process
command-line arguments passed to
your Bash script using special
variables like $1, $2, etc., to access
arguments.

Error Handling:
Learn how to handle errors and exceptions in Bash using conditional statements and error codes.
File I/O:
Explore how to read and write files, manipulate directories, and use standard input/output in Bash scripts.
Pipeline and Redirection:
Understand how to use pipes (|) for chaining commands and redirection (>, >>, <) to manipulate input and output streams.
Practice and Build Projects:
The best way to become proficient in Bash is through practice. Work on real-world automation tasks, system administration scripts, and complex projects.
Documentation and Community:
Refer to the Bash documentation (man bash or online resources) and engage with the Bash community through forums and online resources.

Bash scripting is a powerful tool for automating tasks, managing systems, and running command-line operations efficiently in Unix-like environments.

Creating a simple Bash program

Let's create a simple Bash program that prompts the user for their name and then greets them. This program will demonstrate basic input/output operations in Bash.

Create a Bash Script:

Open a text editor and create a new file with a .sh extension. For example, name it greet.sh.

Write Bash Code:

Inside greet.sh, write the following Bash code:

```bash
#!/bin/bash

# Prompt the user for their name
```

```bash
echo "Enter your name:"

# Read user input
read name

# Greet the user
echo "Hello, $name! Welcome to
Bash!"
```

In this code:

- #!/bin/bash is the shebang line, specifying the path to the Bash interpreter.
- echo "Enter your name:" is used to display the prompt to the user.
- read name reads the user's input and stores it in the variable name.
- echo "Hello, $name! Welcome to Bash!" is used to greet the user by displaying their name.

Make the Script Executable:

Before you can run the Bash script, you need to make it executable. In your terminal, navigate to the directory where you saved your script and run the following command:

```
chmod +x greet.sh
```

Run the Bash Script:
To run the Bash script, you can simply type:

```
./greet.sh
```

Enter Your Name:
You will see the program's output, which prompts you to enter your name. For example:

```
Enter your name:
```

Type your name and press Enter.
View the Output:
After entering your name, the program will greet you. For example:

```
Hello, John! Welcome to Bash!
```

This simple Bash program demonstrates how to prompt the user for input, read and store the input, and display output. Bash is a powerful and versatile scripting language used for automating tasks, system administration, and running command-line operations efficiently in Unix-like environments.

Functional programming languages are a class of programming languages that treat computation as the evaluation of mathematical functions and avoid changing state or mutable data. These languages have gained popularity over the years due to several important benefits they offer:

Readability and Maintainability: Functional programming emphasizes writing code that is clear and concise. With a focus on pure functions (functions that don't have side effects), it's easier to understand what a function does just by looking at its inputs and outputs. This leads to more maintainable codebases and better collaboration among developers.

Modularity: Functional programming promotes modular design, where complex systems are built from small, reusable components. This modularity makes it easier to reason about and maintain large codebases, as well as facilitating code reuse.

Immutability: In functional programming, data is typically immutable, meaning once a value is created, it cannot be changed. This helps prevent bugs caused by unintended changes to data and simplifies reasoning about program behavior.

Predictable Behavior: Functional programs are deterministic, meaning that given the same inputs, they always produce the same outputs. This predictability makes it easier to test and debug code and can lead to more reliable software.

Parallelism and Concurrency: Functional programming encourages code that is naturally parallelizable. Because pure functions don't rely on shared state, they can be executed in parallel without causing race conditions or other concurrency issues. This is particularly important in modern computing environments where multi-core processors are common.

Strong Type Systems: Many functional programming languages have strong type systems that catch errors at compile-time, reducing the likelihood of runtime errors. This leads to more robust and secure code.

Reactive Programming: Functional programming is well-suited for reactive programming, which is essential for building responsive and scalable applications, particularly in web development and real-time systems.

Higher-Order Functions: Functional languages often support higher-order functions, which are functions that can take other functions as arguments or return them as results. This allows for powerful abstractions and expressive programming constructs.

Pure Functions and Testing: Functional programming encourages the use of pure functions, which are easier to test in isolation. This promotes a strong testing culture, leading to higher code quality and reliability.

Expressive and Concise Code: Functional programming languages often provide expressive features like list comprehensions, pattern matching, and concise syntax, allowing developers to write code more elegantly and succinctly.

Mathematical Foundation: Functional programming is rooted in mathematical concepts, which can make it easier to reason about the correctness and performance of algorithms.

Functional Paradigm in Modern Computing: Many modern programming languages, even those traditionally associated with imperative or object-oriented paradigms, have adopted functional programming features or paradigms. Learning functional programming principles can be beneficial for programmers working in a variety of language ecosystems.

While functional programming languages may not be the best choice for every project, they offer valuable tools and approaches that can significantly improve software quality, maintainability, and scalability, making them an important and relevant part of the programming landscape.

Examples of Functional Programming Languages and their specific functions

Functional programming languages are designed to facilitate functional programming, which emphasizes writing programs using pure functions and avoiding mutable state. Here are some examples of functional programming languages and their specific functions:

Haskell:

- Lazy Evaluation: Haskell uses lazy evaluation, which means that expressions are only evaluated when their values are actually needed. This can lead to more efficient and concise code.
- Pattern Matching: Haskell allows pattern matching on data structures, making it easy to destructure and process data.
- Monads: Haskell popularized the concept of monads, which

are used for managing side effects in a purely functional way.

Lisp (Common Lisp, Scheme):
- Homogeneous Code and Data: Lisp treats code and data as lists, which makes it easy to generate and manipulate code within the program.
- Dynamic Typing: Lisp uses dynamic typing, allowing variables to change types at runtime, providing flexibility but also requiring careful type checking.
- Recursion: Lisp encourages recursive programming and supports tail call optimization.

Clojure:
- Immutable Data: Clojure promotes immutable data structures and discourages changing data in place.

- Concurrency: It has built-in support for managing concurrency through software transactional memory (STM).
- Functional Macros: Clojure provides powerful macros that enable the creation of expressive and flexible code.

Erlang:

- Concurrency and Fault Tolerance: Erlang is designed for building highly concurrent and fault-tolerant systems. It excels at handling thousands of lightweight processes, each executing a small function.
- Message Passing: Erlang processes communicate exclusively through message passing, which simplifies concurrent programming.

Scala:

- Functional and Object-Oriented: Scala is a hybrid language that combines functional and object-oriented programming. It supports functional programming constructs like immutability and higher-order functions while also allowing object-oriented development.

- Type Inference: Scala provides strong static typing with type inference, reducing the need for explicit type annotations.

F#:

- Functional-First: F# is a functional-first language in the .NET ecosystem. It supports functional programming paradigms while also allowing object-oriented programming.
- Pattern Matching: F# features pattern matching for concise and expressive code.
- Type Providers: F# introduces type providers, which offer a

form of compile-time
metaprogramming.

Elm:

- Front-End Web Development:
  Elm is a functional
  programming language designed
  for building front-end web
  applications. It emphasizes
  immutability, declarative user
  interfaces, and a strong focus on
  avoiding runtime errors.

PureScript:

- Compile-to-JavaScript:
  PureScript is a strongly-typed
  functional programming
  language that compiles to
  JavaScript, making it suitable
  for web development.
- Type System: It has a powerful
  type system inspired by Haskell,
  including type classes and type
  inference.

Racket:

- Scheme-Based: Racket is a variant of Scheme, which is a Lisp dialect. It is known for its extensibility and is often used for teaching programming languages and building domain-specific languages (DSLs).

These functional programming languages have their own unique features and strengths, but they all share a common emphasis on functional programming principles, including immutability, pure functions, and a focus on expressions over statements. The choice of a functional programming language often depends on the specific requirements of the project and the developer's familiarity with the language.

How to program with Haskell

Programming with Haskell involves writing code using the Haskell programming language. Haskell is a pure functional programming language known for its strong type system, immutability, and mathematical foundations. Here's a step-by-step guide on how to get started with programming in Haskell:

Install Haskell:

Before you start, you need to install Haskell on your system. Haskell has a robust compiler called GHC (Glasgow Haskell Compiler) that you can download and install from the official Haskell website (https://www.haskell.org/platform/). Follow the installation instructions for your specific operating system.

Choose a Text Editor or IDE:

You can write Haskell code using a text editor or an Integrated Development Environment (IDE). Some popular choices for Haskell development include Visual Studio Code with the Haskell plugin, Haskell-specific IDEs like Haskell for

Mac, or dedicated Haskell IDEs like HIE (Haskell IDE Engine).

Create a Haskell File:

Open your chosen text editor or IDE and create a new Haskell file. Haskell files typically have a .hs extension. For example, you can create a file named hello.hs.

Write Haskell Code:

Inside your Haskell file, you can start writing Haskell code. Here's an example of a basic Haskell program that prints "Hello, Haskell!" to the console:

```haskell
main :: IO ()
main = putStrLn "Hello,
Haskell!"
```

In this code:

- main is the main function of your Haskell program.
- :: IO () specifies the type of main. It indicates that main performs input and output operations and has a return type

of (), which means it returns nothing.

- putStrLn is a standard library function for printing a string to the console.

Compile and Run Your Haskell Program:

Open your terminal or command prompt and navigate to the directory where you saved your Haskell file (hello.hs).

Use the GHC compiler to compile your program:

```
ghc hello.hs
```

This command will create an executable file, usually named hello or whatever you specified after the -o flag.

Run your Haskell program:

```
./hello
```

You should see the program's output, which is:

```
Hello, Haskell!
```

Learn Haskell Basics:

- Study the Haskell documentation and tutorials to learn about basic language constructs, including variables, functions, types, pattern matching, and list operations.
- Understand the Haskell type system, including type inference, type classes, and type annotations.

Functional Programming Concepts:

- Familiarize yourself with functional programming principles, such as immutability, pure functions, and higher-order functions.
- Learn how to use monads for managing side effects in a purely functional way.

Explore Advanced Topics:

- Explore advanced Haskell concepts and libraries, including type-level programming, metaprogramming with Template Haskell, and working with libraries for web development, data analysis, and more.

Practice and Build Projects:
The best way to become proficient in Haskell is through practice. Work on projects, solve problems on online platforms like Project Euler or LeetCode, and contribute to open-source Haskell projects.

Community and Resources:
Join the Haskell community, participate in Haskell forums, and explore online resources, books, and tutorials related to Haskell programming.

Haskell is a powerful and expressive programming language that can be used for a wide range of applications, from scientific computing to web development. It has a steep learning curve but offers a unique and rewarding programming experience for those who master it.

Creating a simple Haskell program
Let's create a simple Haskell program that calculates the factorial of a number using a recursive function. This program will demonstrate the basic structure of a Haskell program and how to define functions.

Create a Haskell File:
Open your text editor or Haskell development environment and create a new Haskell file with a .hs extension. For example, name it factorial.hs.
Write Haskell Code:
Inside factorial.hs, write the following Haskell code:

```haskell
-- Define a recursive function
to calculate the factorial of a
number
factorial :: Integer -> Integer
factorial 0 = 1
```

```haskell
factorial n = n * factorial (n - 1)

-- Main function to prompt the user for input and display the result
main :: IO ()
main = do
    putStrLn "Enter a number:"
    input <- getLine
    let number = read input :: Integer
    let result = factorial number
    putStrLn ("The factorial of " ++ show number ++ " is " ++ show result)
```

In this code:

- factorial is a recursive function that calculates the factorial of a number. It uses pattern matching to handle the base case (factorial of 0) and the recursive case.

- main is the main function of your Haskell program. It performs input and output operations.
- putStrLn is used to print a string to the console.
- getLine is used to read a line of input from the user.
- let is used to bind values to variables. We convert the input to an Integer, calculate the factorial, and bind the result to the result variable.
- show is used to convert values to strings for displaying them in the output.

Compile and Run Your Haskell Program:

Open your terminal or command prompt and navigate to the directory where you saved your Haskell file (factorial.hs).

Use the GHC compiler to compile your program:

```
ghc factorial.hs
```
This command will create an executable file, usually named factorial or whatever you specified after the -o flag.
Run your Haskell program:
```
./factorial
```

Enter a Number:
You will see the program's output, which prompts you to enter a number. For example:
```
Enter a number:
```
```
Type a non-negative integer
(e.g., 5) and press Enter.
```
View the Output:
After entering a number, the program will calculate and display the factorial. For example:
```
The factorial of 5 is 120
```

This simple Haskell program demonstrates how to define functions, perform input/output operations, and use recursion.

Haskell's strong type system and purity make it well-suited for writing robust and reliable code.

How to program with Scala

Programming with Scala involves writing code using the Scala programming language, which is a versatile language that combines functional and object-oriented programming paradigms. Scala runs on the Java Virtual Machine (JVM) and is known for its expressive syntax, strong type system, and conciseness. Here's a step-by-step guide on how to get started with programming in Scala:

Install Scala:

Before you start, you need to install Scala on your system. Scala is often bundled with the Scala Build Tool (SBT), which is a popular build tool for Scala projects. You can download the Scala and SBT binaries from the

official Scala website
(https://www.scala-lang.org/downloa
d/) and follow the installation
instructions for your specific operating
system.
Choose a Text Editor or IDE:
You can write Scala code using a text
editor or an Integrated Development
Environment (IDE). Some popular
choices for Scala development include
IntelliJ IDEA with the Scala plugin,
Visual Studio Code with the Metals
extension, and dedicated Scala IDEs
like Scala IDE and Ensime.
Create a Scala File:
Open your chosen text editor or IDE
and create a new Scala file. Scala files
typically have a .scala extension. For
example, you can create a file named
HelloScala.scala.
Write Scala Code:
Inside your Scala file, you can start
writing Scala code. Here's an example

of a basic Scala program that prints
"Hello, Scala!" to the console:

```scala
object HelloScala {
  def main(args: Array[String]):
Unit = {
    println("Hello, Scala!")
  }
}
```

In this code:

- object HelloScala defines an object, which is similar to a class with a single instance. It contains the main method, which serves as the entry point of the program.
- def main(args: Array[String]): Unit = { ... } defines the main method, which takes an array of strings as arguments. Inside the method, println is used to print the greeting to the console.

Compile and Run Your Scala Program:
Open your terminal or command prompt and navigate to the directory

where you saved your Scala file
(HelloScala.scala).
Use the Scala compiler (scalac) to
compile your program:

```
scalac HelloScala.scala
```

This will generate one or more .class
files.
Run your Scala program using the
Scala interpreter (scala):

```
scala HelloScala
```

You should see the program's output,
which is:

```
Hello, Scala!
```

Learn Scala Basics:
- Study the Scala documentation
  and tutorials to learn about basic
  language constructs, including
  variables, functions, classes, and
  pattern matching.
- Understand Scala's strong type
  system, including type inference
  and type annotations.

Functional and Object-Oriented Programming:
- Familiarize yourself with functional programming concepts like immutability, first-class functions, and pattern matching.
- Learn about Scala's support for object-oriented programming, including class hierarchies, inheritance, and traits.

Advanced Topics:
- Explore advanced Scala topics such as pattern matching, for-comprehensions, implicits, and case classes.
- Learn about the Akka library for building highly concurrent and distributed systems in Scala.

Practice and Build Projects:
The best way to become proficient in Scala is through practice. Work on projects, solve problems on online

coding platforms, and contribute to open-source Scala projects.
Community and Resources:
Join the Scala community, participate in Scala forums, and explore online resources, books, and tutorials related to Scala programming.

Scala is a powerful and expressive programming language that can be used for a wide range of applications, from web development to big data processing. Its interoperability with Java makes it a valuable choice for projects in the Java ecosystem.

Creating a simple Scala program

This simple Scala program calculates the sum of even numbers within a given range.
Create a Scala File:
Open your text editor or Scala development environment and create a new Scala file with a .scala

extension. For example, name it EvenSum.scala.

Write Scala Code:

Inside EvenSum.scala, write the following Scala code:

```scala
object EvenSum {
  // Function to calculate the sum of even numbers within a range
  def sumEvenNumbersInRange(start: Int, end: Int): Int = {
    if (start > end) 0
    else if (start % 2 == 0) start + sumEvenNumbersInRange(start + 2, end)
    else sumEvenNumbersInRange(start + 1, end)
  }

  def main(args: Array[String]): Unit = {
```

```scala
    // Prompt the user for input
    println("Enter the start of
the range:")
    val start =
scala.io.StdIn.readInt()

    println("Enter the end of
the range:")
    val end =
scala.io.StdIn.readInt()

    // Calculate and display the
sum of even numbers
    val result =
sumEvenNumbersInRange(start,
end)
    println(s"The sum of even
numbers between $start and $end
is $result")
  }
}
```

In this code:

- object EvenSum defines an object containing the

sumEvenNumbersInRange function and the main method.

- def sumEvenNumbersInRange(start: Int, end: Int): Int defines a recursive function to calculate the sum of even numbers within a given range. It uses pattern matching to handle different cases.
- def main(args: Array[String]): Unit defines the main method, which prompts the user for the start and end of the range, calculates the sum of even numbers, and displays the result.

Compile and Run Your Scala Program: Open your terminal or command prompt and navigate to the directory where you saved your Scala file (EvenSum.scala).

Use the Scala compiler (scalac) to compile your program:

```
scalac EvenSum.scala
```

This will generate one or more .class
files.

Run your Scala program using the
Scala interpreter (scala):

```
scala EvenSum
```

Enter the Range:
You will see the program's output,
which prompts you to enter the start
and end of the range. For example:

```
Enter the start of the range:
```

Type the start (e.g., 2) and press
Enter. Then, enter the end (e.g., 10)
and press Enter.

View the Output:
After entering the range, the program
will calculate and display the sum of
even numbers within that range. For
example:

```
The sum of even numbers between
2 and 10 is 30
```

This Scala program illustrates how to define functions, perform input/output operations, and use recursion to solve a specific problem. It showcases Scala's expressiveness and conciseness in solving real-world problems.

How to program with Elixir

Programming with Elixir involves writing code using the Elixir programming language, which is known for its reliability, fault tolerance, and scalability. Elixir is built on top of the Erlang Virtual Machine (BEAM) and is designed for building distributed and concurrent applications. Here's a step-by-step guide on how to get started with programming in Elixir:

Install Elixir:

Before you start, you need to install Elixir on your system. You can download the latest Elixir version from the official website (https://elixir-lang.org/install.html)

and follow the installation instructions
for your specific operating system.
Choose a Text Editor or IDE:
You can write Elixir code using a text
editor or an Integrated Development
Environment (IDE). Some popular
choices for Elixir development include
Visual Studio Code with the ElixirLS
extension, Atom with the Atom-Elixir
package, and dedicated Elixir IDEs
like IntelliJ IDEA with the Elixir
plugin.
Create an Elixir File:
Open your chosen text editor or IDE
and create a new Elixir file with a .ex
extension. For example, name it
hello.ex.
Write Elixir Code:
Inside hello.ex, write the following
Elixir code for a simple "Hello, Elixir!"
program:

```elixir
IO.puts("Hello, Elixir!")
```

In this code:

- IO.puts/1 is a function that prints a line of text to the standard output.

Compile and Run Your Elixir Program:

Open your terminal or command prompt and navigate to the directory where you saved your Elixir file (hello.ex).

Use the Elixir compiler (elixirc) to compile your program:

```
elixirc hello.ex
```

This will compile your program and generate bytecode files in the same directory.

Run your Elixir program using the Elixir interpreter (elixir):

```
elixir -r hello.ex -e
"Hello.run"
```

You should see the program's output, which is:

```
Hello, Elixir!
```

Learn Elixir Basics:

- Study the Elixir documentation and tutorials to learn about basic language constructs, including variables, functions, modules, and pattern matching.
- Understand Elixir's unique features, such as processes, message passing, and the Actor model for concurrency.

Concurrency and Processes:

- Explore Elixir's concurrency model, which is based on lightweight processes (not OS processes) that communicate via message passing.
- Learn how to create and supervise processes, handle concurrent tasks, and build fault-tolerant systems.

OTP (Open Telecom Platform):

- Familiarize yourself with OTP, which is a set of libraries and design principles for building

robust, fault-tolerant, and distributed systems in Elixir.
- Learn about supervisors, GenServers, and other OTP behaviors.

Advanced Topics:
- Explore advanced Elixir topics, such as metaprogramming with macros, working with Ecto for database interactions, and building web applications using Phoenix.

Practice and Build Projects:
The best way to become proficient in Elixir is through practice. Work on projects, solve problems on online coding platforms, and contribute to open-source Elixir projects.

Community and Resources:
Join the Elixir community, participate in Elixir forums, and explore online resources, books, and tutorials related to Elixir programming.

Elixir is well-suited for building distributed and fault-tolerant systems, making it a valuable language for building scalable and reliable applications, particularly in the areas of web development and real-time systems.

Creating a simple Elixir program

Let's create a simple Elixir program that calculates the factorial of a number using a recursive function. This program will demonstrate the basic structure of an Elixir program and how to define functions.

Create an Elixir File:

Open your text editor or Elixir development environment and create a new Elixir file with a .ex extension. For example, name it factorial.ex.

Write Elixir Code:

Inside factorial.ex, write the following Elixir code:

```elixir
defmodule Factorial do
```

```elixir
  # Define a recursive function
to calculate the factorial of a
number
  def factorial(0), do: 1
  def factorial(n) when n > 0,
do: n * factorial(n - 1)
  def factorial(_), do: "Invalid
input"
end

# Prompt the user for input
IO.puts("Enter a non-negative
integer:")
input = IO.gets("") |>
String.trim() |>
String.to_integer()

# Calculate and display the
factorial
result =
Factorial.factorial(input)
IO.puts("The factorial of
#{input} is #{result}")
```

In this code:

- defmodule Factorial defines a module containing the factorial/1 function and the program logic.
- def factorial(0), do: 1 defines a clause to handle the base case when n is 0. It returns 1.
- def factorial(n) when n > 0, do: n * factorial(n - 1) defines a clause to calculate the factorial recursively for positive n.
- def factorial(_), do: "Invalid input" defines a clause to handle invalid inputs.
- The program starts by prompting the user for input using IO.puts/1 and then reads the input, trims it, and converts it to an integer.
- It calculates the factorial using Factorial.factorial/1 and displays the result.

Run Your Elixir Program:

Open your terminal or command

prompt and navigate to the directory where you saved your Elixir file (factorial.ex).

Run your Elixir program using the elixir command:

```
elixir factorial.ex
```

Enter a Number:
You will see the program's output, which prompts you to enter a non-negative integer. For example:

```
Enter a non-negative integer:
```

Type a non-negative integer (e.g., 5) and press Enter.
View the Output:
After entering a number, the program will calculate and display the factorial. For example:

```
The factorial of 5 is 120
```

This simple Elixir program demonstrates how to define functions, perform input/output operations, and use recursion. Elixir's functional and fault-tolerant nature makes it well-suited for building concurrent and distributed systems, and it is known for its readability and

How to program with Racket

Programming with Racket involves writing code using the Racket programming language, which is a descendant of Scheme and a dialect of Lisp. Racket is known for its simplicity, expressiveness, and support for both functional and imperative programming paradigms. Here's a step-by-step guide on how to get started with programming in Racket:

Install Racket:
Before you start, you need to install Racket on your system. You can download the latest version of Racket from the official website (https://racket-lang.org/download/) and follow the installation instructions for your specific operating system.

Choose a Text Editor or IDE:
You can write Racket code using a text
editor or an Integrated Development
Environment (IDE). Some popular
choices for Racket development
include DrRacket (Racket's official
IDE), Visual Studio Code with the
"Calva" extension, and Sublime Text
with the "Racket" package.

Create a Racket File:
Open your chosen text editor or IDE
and create a new Racket file with a .rkt
extension. For example, name it
hello.rkt.

Write Racket Code:
Inside hello.rkt, write the following
Racket code for a simple "Hello,
Racket!" program:

```
#lang racket

(displayln "Hello, Racket!")
```

In this code:

- #lang racket specifies that you
  are using the Racket language.

- (displayln "Hello, Racket!") is an expression that displays "Hello, Racket!" followed by a newline to the standard output.

Run Your Racket Program:

You can run your Racket program using the DrRacket IDE or from the command line.

Using DrRacket:

- Open DrRacket.
- Open your hello.rkt file.
- Click the "Run" button or press Ctrl+R (or Cmd+R on macOS) to execute the program.
- You should see the program's output in the "Interactions" pane.

Using the Command Line:

- Open your terminal or command prompt and navigate to the directory where you saved your Racket file (hello.rkt).

- Run your Racket program using the racket command:

```
racket hello.rkt
```

View the Output:
You will see the program's output, which is:

```
Hello, Racket!
```

Learn Racket Basics:
- Study the Racket documentation and tutorials to learn about basic language constructs, including variables, functions, and lists.
- Understand Racket's support for functional programming, including first-class functions and higher-order functions.

Advanced Topics:
- Explore advanced Racket topics such as macros, pattern matching, and working with custom data structures.

- Learn about Racket's libraries and packages for various tasks, including web development, graphics, and more.

Practice and Build Projects:

The best way to become proficient in Racket is through practice. Work on projects, solve problems, and explore different aspects of the language.

Community and Resources:

Join the Racket community, participate in Racket forums, and explore online resources, books, and tutorials related to Racket programming.

Racket is a versatile programming language that can be used for a wide range of applications, from writing scripts to building web applications and creating domain-specific languages (DSLs). Its simplicity and expressive syntax make it an excellent choice for both beginners and experienced programmers.

Creating a simple Racket program

Let's create a simple Racket program that calculates the factorial of a number using a recursive function. This program will demonstrate the basic structure of a Racket program and how to define functions.

Create a Racket File:

Open your text editor or DrRacket IDE (if you have it installed) and create a new Racket file with a .rkt extension. For example, name it factorial.rkt.

Write Racket Code:

Inside factorial.rkt, write the following Racket code:

```
;; Define a recursive function
to calculate the factorial of a
number
(define (factorial n)
  (if (= n 0)
      1
```

```scheme
      (* n (factorial (- n
1)))))

;; Prompt the user for input
(display "Enter a non-negative
integer: ")
(flush-output)

;; Read the input as a string
and convert it to an integer
(define input (string->number
(read-line)))

;; Calculate and display the
factorial
(display "The factorial of ")
(display input)
(display " is ")
(display (factorial input))
(newline)
```

In this code:

- (define (factorial n) ...) defines a recursive function to calculate the factorial of an integer n.

- (if (= n 0) ...) is used to handle the base case when n is 0.
- (* n (factorial (- n 1))) calculates the factorial recursively.
- The program starts by prompting the user for input using (display ...) and (flush-output).
- It reads the input as a string, converts it to an integer, calculates the factorial, and displays the result.

Run Your Racket Program:

You can run your Racket program using the DrRacket IDE or from the command line.

Using DrRacket:

- Open DrRacket.
- Open your factorial.rkt file.
- Click the "Run" button or press Ctrl+R (or Cmd+R on macOS) to execute the program.

- You should see the program's output in the "Interactions" pane.

Using the Command Line:

- Open your terminal or command prompt and navigate to the directory where you saved your Racket file (factorial.rkt).
- Run your Racket program using the racket command:

```
racket factorial.rkt
```

-

Enter a Number:

You will see the program's output, which prompts you to enter a non-negative integer. For example:

```
Enter a non-negative integer:
```

Type a non-negative integer (e.g., 5) and press Enter.

View the Output:

After entering a number, the program

will calculate and display the factorial. For example:

```
The factorial of 5 is 120
```

This simple Racket program demonstrates how to define functions, perform input/output operations, and use recursion. Racket's simplicity and support for functional programming make it an excellent choice for both beginners and experienced programmers.

How to program with PureScript

Programming with PureScript involves writing code using the PureScript programming language, which is a strongly typed, purely functional language inspired by Haskell. PureScript compiles to JavaScript, making it suitable for front-end and back-end web development. Here's a step-by-step guide on how to get started with programming in PureScript:

Install Node.js and npm:
Before you start with PureScript, you need to have Node.js and npm (Node Package Manager) installed on your system. You can download and install them from the official website: https://nodejs.org/

Install the PureScript Compiler:
You can install the PureScript compiler globally using npm. Open your terminal or command prompt and run the following command:

```
npm install -g purescript
```

This will install the purescript command-line tool, which you can use to compile PureScript code.

Choose a Text Editor or IDE:
You can write PureScript code using a text editor or an Integrated Development Environment (IDE). Some popular choices for PureScript development include Visual Studio Code with the "PureScript IDE" extension, Atom with the

"language-purescript" package, and the online editor at https://try.purescript.org/.

Create a PureScript Project:

To start a new PureScript project, create a directory for your project and navigate to it in your terminal. For example:

```
mkdir my-purescript-project
cd my-purescript-project
```

Initialize the Project:

Initialize a new npm project in your PureScript project directory by running the following command and following the prompts:

```
npm init
```

This will create a package.json file. Install PureScript Dependencies: You'll need some PureScript dependencies for your project. Install the PureScript compiler and a package manager called spago using npm:

```
npm install purescript spago
--save-dev
```

Additionally, you may want to install PureScript packages for libraries or frameworks you plan to use, such as purescript-prelude for the standard library.

Write PureScript Code:

Create a PureScript source file with a .purs extension in your project directory. For example, name it Main.purs.

Inside Main.purs, you can start writing PureScript code. Here's a simple "Hello, PureScript!" program:

```
module Main where

import Prelude

main :: Effect Unit
main = do
  log "Hello, PureScript!"
```

In this code:

- module Main where specifies the module name.
- import Prelude imports the standard library.
- main :: Effect Unit defines the main function with a side effect of type Effect.
- log is used to print a message to the console.

Compile Your PureScript Code:
Open your terminal and navigate to your project directory.
Use the spago package manager to build your PureScript project:

```
npx spago build
```

This command will compile your PureScript code and produce JavaScript output in the output directory.
Run Your PureScript Code:
You can execute your PureScript code using Node.js. For example:

```
node -e
"require('./output/Main').main()
"
```

This command runs the main function defined in your PureScript code.

Learn PureScript Basics:

- Study the PureScript documentation and tutorials to learn about basic language constructs, including type annotations, functions, and records.
- Understand PureScript's strong type system and type inference.

Advanced Topics:

- Explore advanced PureScript topics such as monads, type classes, and writing type-safe web applications using libraries like purescript-halogen for front-end development.

Practice and Build Projects:

The best way to become proficient in PureScript is through practice. Work on projects, solve problems, and explore different aspects of the language.

Community and Resources: Join the PureScript community, participate in forums, and explore online resources, books, and tutorials related to PureScript programming.

PureScript is a powerful language for functional programming that compiles to JavaScript, making it a valuable tool for modern web development, particularly for projects where strong static typing and functional programming are desired.

Creating a simple PureScript program

Let's create a simple PureScript program that calculates the factorial of a number and demonstrates basic PureScript syntax and functional programming concepts.
Follow these steps:

Initialize a New PureScript Project:
If you haven't already, create a new
directory for your PureScript project
and navigate to it in your terminal.

```
mkdir my-purescript-project
cd my-purescript-project
```

Initialize the Project:
Initialize an npm project in your
project directory:

```
npm init
```

Follow the prompts to create a
package.json file.

Install PureScript Dependencies:
Install the PureScript compiler
(purescript) and the package manager
(spago) as development dependencies:

```
npm install purescript spago
--save-dev
```

Initialize Spago:
Initialize the project with spago:

```
npx spago init
```

This command will create a spago.dhall configuration file and set up your project for PureScript development.

Create a PureScript Source File: Inside your project directory, create a new PureScript source file with a .purs extension. For example, name it Main.purs.

Write PureScript Code: Inside Main.purs, write the following PureScript code to calculate the factorial of a number:

```
module Main where

import Prelude

-- Define a factorial function using recursion
factorial :: Int -> Int
factorial 0 = 1
factorial n = n * factorial (n - 1)
```

```
main :: Effect Unit
main = do
  let num = 5
  log $ "The factorial of " <>
show num <> " is " <> show
(factorial num)
```

In this code:

- module Main where specifies the module name.
- import Prelude imports the standard library.
- factorial is a recursive function that calculates the factorial of an integer.
- main is the main function that calculates and logs the factorial of a specific number (in this case, 5).

Build Your PureScript Project:
Build your PureScript project using spago:

```
npx spago build
```

Run Your PureScript Program:

You can execute your PureScript program using Node.js:

```
node -e
"require('./output/Main').main()
"
```

This command will run the main function defined in your PureScript code, and you should see the output:

```
The factorial of 5 is 120
```

That's it! You've created a simple PureScript program that calculates the factorial of a number. This example demonstrates how to define functions, perform input/output operations, and work with basic PureScript syntax. You can continue to explore more advanced PureScript topics and libraries for functional programming and web development.

How to program with Elm

Programming with Elm involves writing code using the Elm programming language, which is a functional, statically typed language known for building web applications with a strong emphasis on reliability and maintainability. Elm compiles to JavaScript, making it a popular choice for front-end web development. Here's a step-by-step guide on how to get started with programming in Elm:

Install Elm:

Before you start, you need to have Elm installed on your system. You can download the latest Elm version from the official website (https://elm-lang.org/), and installation instructions are available there for your specific operating system.

Choose a Text Editor or IDE:

You can write Elm code using a text editor or an Integrated Development Environment (IDE). Some popular

choices for Elm development include Visual Studio Code with the "Elm" extension, Sublime Text with the "Elm Language" package, and Atom with the "language-elm" package.
Create an Elm Project:
To start a new Elm project, create a directory for your project and navigate to it in your terminal. For example:

```
mkdir my-elm-project
cd my-elm-project
```

Initialize the Project:
Initialize a new Elm project by running the following command:

```
elm init
```

This will create an elm.json configuration file and a src directory for your Elm source code.
Write Elm Code:
Inside the src directory, create a new Elm source file with a .elm extension. For example, name it Main.elm.
Inside Main.elm, you can start writing

Elm code. Here's a simple "Hello, Elm!" program:

```elm
module Main exposing (..)

import Html exposing (text)

main =
    text "Hello, Elm!"
```

In this code:

- module Main exposing (..) specifies the module name and exposes all functions and values.
- import Html exposing (text) imports the text function from the Elm Html module.
- main is a value that represents the content of your web page. In this case, it's a simple text message.

Compile Your Elm Code:

Open your terminal and navigate to your project directory.

Use the Elm compiler (elm make) to compile your Elm code to JavaScript:

```
elm make src/Main.elm
--output=elm.js
```

This command will generate a elm.js JavaScript file in your project directory.

Create an HTML File:

Create an HTML file (e.g., index.html) in your project directory to display the Elm application:

```html
<!DOCTYPE html>
<html>
<head>
    <title>My Elm App</title>
</head>
<body>
    <div id="elm-container"></div>
    <script src="elm.js"></script>
    <script>
        Elm.Main.init({
            node: document.getElementById('elm-container')
```

```
      });
    </script>
</body>
</html>
```

This HTML file includes the elm.js script and initializes the Elm application in a div with the ID elm-container.

Run Your Elm Program:

Open the HTML file (index.html) in a web browser. You should see the "Hello, Elm!" message displayed in your web page.

Learn Elm Basics:

- Study the Elm documentation and tutorials to learn about basic language constructs, including functions, records, and type annotations.
- Understand Elm's strong type system and the concept of The Elm Architecture (TEA) for building interactive applications.

Advanced Topics:

- Explore advanced Elm topics such as message passing, model-view-update (MVU) architecture, and working with Elm libraries for routing, HTTP requests, and more.

Practice and Build Projects:
The best way to become proficient in Elm is through practice. Work on projects, solve problems, and explore different aspects of the language.

Community and Resources:
Join the Elm community, participate in Elm forums, and explore online resources, books, and tutorials related to Elm programming.

Elm is a language that emphasizes developer productivity and robustness, making it an excellent choice for building web applications that require reliability and maintainability.

Creating a simple Elm program

Let's create a simple Elm program that displays a "Hello, Elm!" message in a web browser. Follow these steps:

Create an Elm Project:

If you haven't already, create a new directory for your Elm project and navigate to it in your terminal:

```
mkdir my-elm-project
cd my-elm-project
```

Initialize the Project:

Initialize a new Elm project by running the following command:

```
elm init
```

This will create an elm.json configuration file and a src directory for your Elm source code.

Create an Elm Source File:

Inside the src directory, create a new Elm source file with a .elm extension. For example, name it Main.elm.

Write Elm Code:
Inside Main.elm, write the following
Elm code:

```elm
module Main exposing (..)

import Browser
import Html exposing (Html, div,
text)

main =
    Browser.sandbox { init =
init, update = update, view =
view }

type Model =
    { message : String }

init : Model
init =
    { message = "Hello, Elm!" }

type Msg =
    NoOp
```

```elm
update : Msg -> Model -> Model
update msg model =
    case msg of
        NoOp ->
            model


view : Model -> Html Msg
view model =
    div [] [ text model.message
]
```

In this code:

- module Main exposing (..) specifies the module name and exposes all functions and values.
- We import the Browser module for creating Elm applications and the Html module for rendering HTML.
- main initializes a simple Elm application with a model, update function, and view function.
- Model defines the data structure for our application's state, including a message field.

- init initializes the initial model.
- Msg defines the possible messages (actions) that can be sent to the update function.
- update handles messages by returning a new model.
- view generates the HTML to be displayed, which includes the message from the model.

Compile Your Elm Code:

Open your terminal and navigate to your project directory.

Use the Elm compiler (elm make) to compile your Elm code to JavaScript:

```
elm make src/Main.elm
--output=elm.js
```

This command will generate an elm.js JavaScript file in your project directory.

Create an HTML File:

Create an HTML file (e.g., index.html) in your project directory to display the Elm application:

```html
<!DOCTYPE html>
<html>
<head>
    <title>My Elm App</title>
</head>
<body>
    <div
id="elm-container"></div>
    <script
src="elm.js"></script>
    <script>
        var app =
Elm.Main.init({
            node:
document.getElementById('elm-con
tainer')
        });
    </script>
</body>
</html>
```

This HTML file includes the elm.js
script and initializes the Elm
application in a div with the ID
elm-container.

Run Your Elm Program:
Open the HTML file (index.html) in a
web browser. You should see the
"Hello, Elm!" message displayed on
the web page.

That's it! You've created a simple Elm
program that displays a message in a web
browser. Elm's architecture, which includes
the model, update, and view functions, is
designed for building maintainable and
reliable web applications. You can continue
to explore more advanced Elm concepts and
libraries for building interactive web
applications.

How to program with F#

Programming with F# involves writing code
using the F# programming language, which
is a functional-first, multi-paradigm
language developed by Microsoft. F# runs
on the .NET platform and is particularly
well-suited for tasks such as data analysis,
web development, and scripting. Here's a

step-by-step guide on how to get started
with programming in F#:

Install the .NET SDK:

Before you start, you need to have the
.NET SDK (Software Development
Kit) installed on your system. You can
download and install it from the
official website:
https://dotnet.microsoft.com/downlo
ad/dotnet.
Choose a Text Editor or IDE:
You can write F# code using a text
editor or an Integrated Development
Environment (IDE). Some popular
choices for F# development include
Visual Studio Code with the "Ionide"
extension, Visual Studio with F# tools,
and JetBrains Rider.
Create an F# Project:
To start a new F# project, create a
directory for your project and navigate
to it in your terminal. For example:

```
mkdir my-fsharp-project
cd my-fsharp-project
```

Initialize the Project:
Initialize a new F# project by running
the following command:

```
dotnet new console -lang F#
```

This command will create a new F#
console application.

Write F# Code:
Inside your project directory, you'll
find a Program.fs file that contains the
main F# code. You can start writing
your F# code there. Here's a simple
"Hello, F#!" program:

```
open System


[<EntryPoint>]
let main argv =
    Console.WriteLine("Hello,
F#!")
    0 // Return an integer exit
code
```

In this code:

- open System brings in
  functionality from the System

namespace, which includes the
Console class.

- `[<EntryPoint>]` is an
  attribute that indicates the entry
  point of the program.
- main is the entry point function,
  which prints a message and
  returns an integer exit code.

Compile and Run Your F# Program:
Open your terminal and navigate to
your project directory.
Use the .NET CLI (Command Line
Interface) to build and run your F#
program:

```
dotnet build
dotnet run
```

You should see the "Hello, F#!"
message displayed in your terminal.

Learn F# Basics:

- Study the F# documentation
  and tutorials to learn about basic
  language constructs, including
  functions, types, and pattern
  matching.

- Understand F#'s functional
  programming features,
  including immutability,
  first-class functions, and type
  inference.

Advanced Topics:

- Explore advanced F# topics such
  as async programming,
  computation expressions
  (similar to monads), and
  working with data using F# type
  providers.

Practice and Build Projects:

The best way to become proficient in
F# is through practice. Work on
projects, solve problems, and explore
different aspects of the language.
Community and Resources:
Join the F# community, participate in
F# forums, and explore online
resources, books, and tutorials related
to F# programming.

F# is a versatile language that combines
functional and object-oriented

programming paradigms. It is well-suited for a wide range of tasks, from data analysis and scripting to web development and server-side programming on the .NET platform.

Creating a simple F# program

Let's create a simple F# program that calculates the factorial of a number using a recursive function. This program will demonstrate the basic structure of an F# program and how to define functions. Follow these steps:

Create an F# Project:
If you haven't already, create a new directory for your F# project and navigate to it in your terminal:

```
mkdir my-fsharp-program
cd my-fsharp-program
```

Initialize the Project:
Initialize a new F# console application by running the following command:

```
dotnet new console -lang F#
```
This command will create a new F# console application project.

Write F# Code:

Open the Program.fs file in your project directory and replace the existing code with the following F# code:

```fsharp
open System

let rec factorial n =
    if n <= 1 then 1
    else n * factorial (n - 1)

[<EntryPoint>]
let main argv =
    let num = 5
    let result = factorial num
    printfn "The factorial of %d is %d" num result
    0 // Return an integer exit code
```

In this code:

- open System brings in functionality from the System namespace, which includes the printfn function for formatted output.
- factorial is a recursive function that calculates the factorial of an integer n.
- [<EntryPoint>] is an attribute that indicates the entry point of the program.
- main is the entry point function, which calculates the factorial of a specific number (in this case, 5) and prints the result.

Compile and Run Your F# Program:

Open your terminal and navigate to your project directory.

Use the .NET CLI to build and run your F# program:

```
dotnet build
dotnet run
```

You should see the following output in your terminal:

```
The factorial of 5 is 120
```

The program has successfully calculated and displayed the factorial of 5.

That's it! You've created a simple F# program that calculates the factorial of a number using a recursive function. This example demonstrates how to define functions, perform input/output operations, and work with basic F# syntax. F# combines functional and imperative programming paradigms and is known for its concise and expressive code. You can explore more advanced features and libraries as you continue your journey with F# programming.

How to program with Erlang

Programming with Erlang involves writing code using the Erlang programming language, which is a functional and concurrent programming language designed for building highly scalable, fault-tolerant, and distributed systems. Erlang is particularly well-suited for building real-time and telecommunications applications. Here's a step-by-step guide on how to get started with programming in Erlang:

Install Erlang/OTP:
Before you start, you need to have Erlang/OTP installed on your system. You can download and install it from the official website: https://www.erlang.org/downloads.
Choose a Text Editor or IDE:
You can write Erlang code using a text editor or an Integrated Development Environment (IDE). Some popular choices for Erlang development include Visual Studio Code with the "erlang-ls" extension, Emacs with the "erlang-mode," and IntelliJ IDEA with the "Erlang" plugin.

Start an Erlang Shell:
To write and execute Erlang code interactively, you can start an Erlang shell. Open your terminal or command prompt and run the erl command:

```
erl
```

You will enter the Erlang shell, where you can execute Erlang commands and write Erlang programs interactively.
Write Erlang Code:
You can write Erlang code directly in the Erlang shell or create separate Erlang source files with a .erl extension. Here's a simple "Hello, Erlang!" program:
Create a file named hello.erl with the following content:

```
-module(hello).
-export([world/0]).

world() ->
    io:format("Hello, Erlang!~n").
```

In this code:

- `-module(hello).` specifies the module name as hello.
- `-export([world/0]).` exports the world/0 function so that it can be called from outside the module.
- `world() -> ...` defines the world function, which prints "Hello, Erlang!" using io:format/1.

Compile Your Erlang Code:
To compile an Erlang source file (e.g., hello.erl) into bytecode, run the following command in the Erlang shell:

```
c(hello).
```

This will compile the hello.erl file and produce a hello.beam bytecode file in the current directory.

Execute Erlang Functions:
You can execute Erlang functions from the shell or by loading them into the shell. For example, to execute the

world/0 function from the hello module, run:

```
hello:world().
```

You should see the "Hello, Erlang!" message printed in the shell.

Learn Erlang Basics:

- Study the Erlang documentation and tutorials to learn about basic language constructs, including functions, modules, and processes.
- Understand Erlang's concurrency model and how processes communicate through message passing.

Advanced Topics:

- Explore advanced Erlang topics such as supervision trees, distributed programming, and building fault-tolerant systems using OTP (Open Telecom Platform).

Practice and Build Projects:
The best way to become proficient in

Erlang is through practice. Work on projects, solve problems, and explore different aspects of the language, especially focusing on concurrent and distributed programming.
Community and Resources:
Join the Erlang community, participate in forums, and explore online resources, books, and tutorials related to Erlang programming.
Erlang is a unique programming language known for its fault-tolerant and distributed capabilities. It is commonly used in industries such as telecommunications and finance for building highly available and scalable systems.

Creating a simple Erlang program

Let's create a simple Erlang program that defines a module and a function to find the sum of integers in a list. Here are the steps:

Create an Erlang Source File:
Create a new Erlang source file with a
.erl extension. For example, name it
sum_list.erl.
Write Erlang Code:
Open the sum_list.erl file and add the
following Erlang code:

```erlang
-module(sum_list).
-export([sum/1]).


sum([]) ->
    0;
sum([H | T]) ->
    H + sum(T).
```

In this code:

- -module(sum_list). specifies the
  module name as sum_list.
- -export([sum/1]). exports the
  sum/1 function so that it can be
  called from outside the module.
- sum/1 is a recursive function
  that takes a list of integers as its
  argument. It calculates the sum

of the integers in the list using pattern matching.

Compile Your Erlang Code:

To compile the sum_list.erl file into bytecode, open a terminal or command prompt and navigate to the directory containing your Erlang source file. Then, run the following command:

```
erlc sum_list.erl
```

This will generate a sum_list.beam file in the same directory.

Start an Erlang Shell:

Start an Erlang shell by running the erl command in your terminal:

```
erl
```

You will enter the Erlang shell, where you can load and execute Erlang code.

Load and Execute Your Erlang Module:

Inside the Erlang shell, load your sum_list module using the following command:

```
c(sum_list).
```

You should see output indicating that the module has been successfully compiled and loaded.

Calculate the Sum:

Now that your module is loaded, you can use it to calculate the sum of a list of integers. For example, find the sum of the list [1, 2, 3, 4, 5] by running the following command in the Erlang shell:

```
sum_list:sum([1, 2, 3, 4, 5]).
```

The result should be displayed in the shell:

```
15
```

This indicates the sum of the integers in the list.

That's it! You've created a simple Erlang program that calculates the sum of integers in a list. This example demonstrates how to define functions, compile and execute Erlang code, and use recursion for list processing. Feel free to modify the program or explore more advanced Erlang concepts and libraries as you continue your journey with Erlang programming.

How to program with ClojureLisp

Programming with Clojure, often referred to as Clojure Lisp, involves writing code using the Clojure programming language. Clojure is a modern, functional Lisp dialect that runs on the Java Virtual Machine (JVM) and is known for its simplicity, immutability, and expressive syntax. Here's a step-by-step guide on how to get started with programming in Clojure:

Install Clojure:

Before you start, you need to have Clojure installed on your system. You can use Leiningen, a popular build and project management tool for Clojure, to create and run Clojure projects. To install Leiningen, follow the instructions on the official website: https://leiningen.org/#install

Choose a Text Editor or IDE:
You can write Clojure code using a text editor or an Integrated Development Environment (IDE). Some popular choices for Clojure development include Visual Studio Code with the "Calva" extension, Cursive for IntelliJ IDEA, and Emacs with the "CIDER" package.

`Create a Clojure Project:`
To start a new Clojure project, use Leiningen to create a project template. Open your terminal and run the following command:

```
lein new my-clojure-project
```

This will create a new Clojure project in a directory named my-clojure-project.
Write Clojure Code:
Inside your project directory, you'll find a src directory where you can place your Clojure source files. Open the core.clj file (or create a new .clj file) and start writing Clojure code.

Here's a simple "Hello, Clojure!"
program:

```clojure
(ns my-clojure-project.core
  (:gen-class))

(defn -main
  "I don't do a whole lot."
  [& args]
  (println "Hello, Clojure!"))
```

In this code:

- `(ns my-clojure-project.core (:gen-class))` declares the namespace and enables AOT (Ahead-of-Time) compilation.
- `(defn -main ...)` defines the -main function, which is the entry point of the program. It prints "Hello, Clojure!" to the console.

Run Your Clojure Program:

Open your terminal, navigate to your project directory (my-clojure-project), and run your Clojure program using Leiningen:

```
lein run
```

You should see the "Hello, Clojure!" message displayed in your terminal.

Learn Clojure Basics:

- Study the Clojure documentation and tutorials to learn about basic language constructs, including functions, data structures, and immutability.
- Understand Clojure's functional programming features, such as first-class functions, higher-order functions, and immutability.

Advanced Topics:

- Explore advanced Clojure topics such as macros, concurrency, and working with Java libraries and interop.

Practice and Build Projects:

The best way to become proficient in

Clojure is through practice. Work on projects, solve problems, and explore different aspects of the language.
Community and Resources:
Join the Clojure community, participate in Clojure forums, and explore online resources, books, and tutorials related to Clojure programming.

Clojure is a powerful, modern Lisp dialect that combines functional programming with the benefits of the JVM ecosystem. It is known for its succinct and expressive code, making it an excellent choice for building robust and scalable applications.

Creating a simple ClojureLisp program

Let's create a simple Clojure program that calculates the factorial of a number using a recursive function. This program will demonstrate the basic structure of a Clojure program and how to define functions.

Follow these steps:

Create a Clojure Project:

If you haven't already, create a new Clojure project directory. You can use Leiningen to create a project. Open your terminal and run the following command:

```
lein new my-clojure-program
```

This command will create a new Clojure project in a directory named my-clojure-program.

Write Clojure Code:

Inside your project directory, navigate to the src/my_clojure_program directory. Open the core.clj file and replace its contents with the following Clojure code:

```clojure
(ns my-clojure-program.core)

(defn factorial [n]
  (if (<= n 1)
    1
    (* n (factorial (- n 1)))))
```

```clojure
(defn -main [& args]
  (let [num 5]
    (println (str "The factorial
of " num " is " (factorial
num)))))
```

In this code:

- `(ns my-clojure-program.core)` declares the namespace for the program.
- `(defn factorial [n] ...)` defines a recursive factorial function that calculates the factorial of a number n.
- `(defn -main [& args] ...)` defines the -main function, which is the entry point of the program. It calculates and prints the factorial of the number 5.

Run Your Clojure Program:

Open your terminal, navigate to your project directory

(my-clojure-program), and run your Clojure program using Leiningen:

```
lein run
```

You should see the following output displayed in your terminal:

```
The factorial of 5 is 120
```

This indicates that the program has successfully calculated and printed the factorial of 5.

This example demonstrates how to define functions, use conditional statements, and execute a Clojure program using Leiningen. Clojure's functional and concise syntax makes it well-suited for various programming tasks. You can continue to explore more advanced Clojure features and libraries as you dive deeper into Clojure programming.

Domain-Specific Languages (DSLs) play a crucial role in software development and various other domains due to their unique benefits and importance. Here are some key reasons why DSLs are important:

Increased Productivity: DSLs are designed to solve specific problems within a well-defined domain. By providing abstractions and language constructs tailored to that domain, DSLs can significantly boost developer productivity. Developers can work at a higher level of abstraction, which reduces the need to deal with low-level details and boilerplate code.

Improved Communication: DSLs enable better communication between domain experts and developers. They provide a common language that both technical and non-technical stakeholders can use to express requirements, specifications, and constraints. This reduces misunderstandings and ensures that software solutions align with domain-specific needs.

Higher Quality Software: DSLs can enforce domain-specific constraints and rules, making it more difficult to introduce errors or vulnerabilities in the software. By reducing the gap between domain knowledge and code implementation, DSLs contribute to the development of higher quality, more reliable software systems.

Faster Development Cycles: DSLs allow developers to express domain-specific concepts and logic more succinctly. This leads to shorter development cycles and quicker time-to-market for software solutions in specialized domains. Rapid development is especially critical in competitive industries.

Ease of Maintenance: Software written using DSLs tends to be more maintainable. Since DSL code closely resembles the domain's language and concepts, updates and modifications are easier to understand and implement. This reduces the risk of introducing regressions or errors during maintenance.

Reusable Components: DSLs can facilitate the creation of reusable components and libraries specific to a particular domain. These components can be shared across projects within the same domain, promoting consistency and reducing development effort.

Simplified Testing and Validation: DSLs can provide built-in support for domain-specific testing and validation, making it easier to verify that software systems meet the required domain-specific criteria. Automated testing tools and techniques can be customized for DSLs to ensure correctness and compliance.

Enhanced Tooling: DSLs often lead to specialized tooling and development environments tailored to the domain. These tools can offer features such as code generation, validation, code completion, and domain-specific visualizations, further improving productivity.

Separation of Concerns: DSLs allow developers to focus on domain-specific concerns without cluttering the codebase with irrelevant details. This separation of concerns makes the code more understandable, maintainable, and extensible.

Support for Domain Experts: DSLs empower domain experts who may not have a programming background to define, manipulate, and interact with domain-specific models and data. This democratizes the development process and enables subject matter experts to have a direct impact on software solutions.

Regulatory Compliance: In domains with strict regulatory requirements (e.g., healthcare, finance), DSLs can enforce compliance by incorporating domain-specific rules and checks into the software, helping organizations adhere to legal and industry standards.

Innovation and Competitive Advantage: DSLs can drive innovation by enabling organizations to model and implement unique approaches, strategies, or processes specific to their domain. This can lead to a competitive advantage and differentiation in the marketplace.

In summary, Domain-Specific Languages are important tools that facilitate efficient, accurate, and maintainable software development within specialized domains. They bridge the gap between domain knowledge and code, leading to higher-quality software, faster development cycles, and improved collaboration between domain experts and developers.

**Examples of Domain-Specific
Languages and their specific
functions**

Domain-Specific Languages (DSLs) can be
found in various domains, each serving a
specific purpose tailored to that domain's
requirements. Here are some examples of
DSLs and their specific functions in
different domains:

**SQL (Structured Query
Language):**

- **Domain**: Database
  Management
- **Function**: SQL is used to query,
  insert, update, and manage data
  in relational databases. It
  provides domain-specific
  constructs for expressing
  database operations, such as
  SELECT statements for data
  retrieval.

**HTML (Hypertext Markup
Language):**

- Domain: Web Development

- Function: HTML is used for creating the structure and content of web pages. It defines elements and tags specific to web document layout and presentation.

CSS (Cascading Style Sheets):
- Domain: Web Development
- Function: CSS is used to describe the presentation and styling of web pages. It provides domain-specific properties and values for controlling fonts, colors, layout, and responsive design.

LaTeX:
- Domain: Typesetting and Document Preparation
- Function: LaTeX is a DSL for typesetting documents, particularly in the fields of academia and publishing. It offers domain-specific markup for creating documents with

complex structures,
mathematical formulas, and
bibliographies.

Regular Expressions (Regex):
- Domain: Text Pattern Matching
- Function: Regular expressions
  provide a DSL for specifying
  patterns in text strings. They are
  used in text processing tasks,
  such as searching, validation,
  and data extraction.

YAML (YAML Ain't Markup Language):
- **Domain**: Configuration Files
- **Function**: YAML is a DSL for
  configuration files. It offers a
  human-readable format to
  define settings and
  configurations for software
  applications.

PromQL (Prometheus Query Language):
- **Domain**: Monitoring and
  Alerting

- **Function**: PromQL is used to query and analyze metrics collected by the Prometheus monitoring system. It provides a DSL for expressing queries and alerting conditions.

Verilog and VHDL:
- Domain: Hardware Description
- Function: Verilog and VHDL are DSLs used for hardware description and digital circuit design. They enable engineers to specify the behavior and structure of electronic circuits.

MDX (Multidimensional Expressions):
- Domain: Business Intelligence and Analytics
- Function: MDX is used to query and analyze multidimensional data models, such as those used in OLAP (Online Analytical Processing) systems. It provides

a DSL for aggregating and slicing data.

Gherkin:

- **Domain**: Behavior-Driven Development (BDD)
- **Function**: Gherkin is a DSL for specifying behavior and acceptance criteria of software features. It is often used with tools like Cucumber to write human-readable tests.

DSLs for Financial Instruments (e.g., FIX Protocol):

- **Domain**: Financial Services
- **Function**: DSLs are used to describe financial instruments, trading strategies, and order routing. FIX (Financial Information Exchange) Protocol is a DSL for real-time electronic communication of financial trade-related information.

Robot Framework DSL:

- Domain: Test Automation

- Function: Robot Framework is a DSL for specifying and executing automated test cases. It offers keywords and syntax tailored for testing and test automation.

These examples illustrate the diverse range of DSLs across various domains, from databases and web development to typesetting, hardware design, and financial services. DSLs enhance productivity and effectiveness within their respective domains by providing specialized syntax and semantics for specific tasks and industries.

Programming with HTML

HTML (Hypertext Markup Language) is a markup language used for creating the structure and content of web pages. HTML documents consist of tags and elements that define the structure and content of a web page. To program with HTML, you need to follow these fundamental steps:

Set Up Your Environment:

- HTML does not require any specific development environment or compiler. You can write HTML code using a simple text editor like Notepad (on Windows) or any code editor, such as Visual Studio Code, Sublime Text, or Atom.

Create an HTML Document:

- Every HTML page starts with a basic structure. You should include the following lines at the beginning of your HTML file:

```
<!DOCTYPE html>
<html>
<head>
    <title>Page Title</title>
</head>
<body>
    <!-- Your content goes here
-->
</body>
</html>
```

- `<!DOCTYPE html>`: This declaration defines the document type and version of HTML. For modern web development, it should be HTML5.
- `<html>`: The root element that encapsulates the entire HTML document.
- `<head>`: Contains meta-information about the document, such as the title of the page and links to external resources like stylesheets and scripts.
- `<title>`: Sets the title of the web page, which appears in the browser's title bar or tab.
- `<body>`: Contains the main content of the web page.

Add Content and Elements:

- Use HTML tags to structure your content. HTML tags are

enclosed in angle brackets <tag> and can have attributes to provide additional information. Here are some commonly used HTML tags:

- `<h1>`, `<h2>`, `<h3>`, ... `<h6>`: Headings
- `<p>`: Paragraphs
- `<a>`: Links
- `<img>`: Images
- `<ul>` and `<ol>`: Unordered and Ordered Lists
- `<li>`: List Items
- `<div>` and `<span>`: Generic container elements
- `<table>`, `<tr>`, `<td>`, `<th>`: Tables
- `<form>`, `<input>`, `<button>`, `<select>`: Forms and form elements

- Here's an example of adding a heading and a paragraph to your HTML document:

```
<h1>Welcome to My Website</h1>
<p>This is a simple example of
an HTML page.</p>
```

-

Save Your HTML File:

- Save your HTML code with an .html file extension, such as index.html. Ensure that you save it in a location accessible via a web server if you plan to publish it online.

View Your HTML Page:

- Open your HTML file in a web browser to see how it renders. Right-click on the HTML file and select "Open with..." to choose your preferred web browser.

Edit and Iterate:

- Continue editing and refining your HTML code to create the desired structure and content for your web page. Experiment with different HTML tags and attributes to achieve the desired layout and appearance.

Learn HTML Syntax and Tags:

- To become proficient in HTML programming, study the HTML syntax, and explore the full range of HTML tags and attributes available. Numerous online tutorials, courses, and documentation resources are available to help you learn HTML in-depth.

HTML serves as the backbone of web development, providing the structure and content for web pages. As you become more comfortable with HTML, you can further enhance your web pages by incorporating CSS (Cascading Style Sheets) for styling and JavaScript for interactivity.

Programming with SQL

Programming with SQL (Structured Query Language) involves writing queries and commands to interact with relational databases. SQL is used for tasks like data retrieval, data manipulation, and database management. Here's a step-by-step guide on how to program with SQL:

Choose a Database System:

- Before you start, you need access to a relational database system like MySQL, PostgreSQL, Microsoft SQL Server, Oracle, or SQLite. Install and set up the database system on your machine or use a cloud-based database service.

Connect to the Database:

- Use a database client or command-line tool to connect to the database system. You'll need the hostname, port, username, and password to establish a connection.

Create a Database (Optional):

- If you're working with a new project, you might need to create a new database. SQL provides commands for database creation, such as CREATE DATABASE in MySQL or PostgreSQL.

Use SQL Statements:

- SQL consists of various types of statements. Here are some commonly used ones:

- **Data Query Language (DQL):** Use SELECT statements to retrieve data from a database. For example, to retrieve all rows from a table called customers:

```
SELECT * FROM customers;
```

- **Data Definition Language (DDL):**

    DDL statements are used to define and modify

database structures.
Examples include creating
tables (CREATE TABLE),
altering tables (ALTER
TABLE), and deleting
tables (DROP TABLE).

- **Data Manipulation
  Language (DML):**
  DML statements are used
  to manipulate data.
  Examples include
  inserting data into tables
  (INSERT INTO), updating
  data (UPDATE), and
  deleting data (DELETE
  FROM).

- **Data Control Language
  (DCL):**
  DCL statements control
  access to data. Examples
  include granting and
  revoking permissions
  (GRANT and REVOKE).

Write SQL Queries:

- Write SQL queries to retrieve
  and manipulate data as per your
  project requirements. For
  example, to retrieve customers
  with a specific name from the
  customers table:

```
SELECT * FROM customers WHERE
name = 'John Doe';
```

Execute SQL Statements:

- Run your SQL statements using
  the database client or
  command-line tool. The tool will
  send the SQL statement to the
  database, which will process it
  and return the results.

Inspect and Analyze Results:

- Review the results returned by
  your SQL queries or statements.
  Depending on the tool you're
  using, results may be displayed
  in tabular format. You can also
  export data or save query results
  to a file.

Practice and Learn SQL:

- SQL is a powerful language, and proficiency comes with practice. To become proficient in SQL, work on complex queries, join tables, aggregate data, and explore more advanced SQL features like subqueries and indexing.

Learn Database Design (Optional):

- Understanding database design principles is essential for working with SQL effectively. Learn about database normalization, primary keys, foreign keys, and entity-relationship diagrams (ERDs).

Handle Errors and Transactions (Advanced):

- Learn to handle errors gracefully in SQL, and understand the concept of database transactions for ensuring data integrity.

Refer to Documentation and Tutorials:

- Use the documentation and tutorials provided by your chosen database system to learn more about its specific SQL dialect and features.

Backup and Security (Important):

- Familiarize yourself with database backup and security practices to protect your data and ensure data recovery in case of unforeseen issues.

SQL is a foundational skill for working with relational databases, and it's widely used in software development, data analysis, and database administration roles. As you gain experience, you can work on more complex SQL queries and tasks, making you a proficient SQL programmer.

How to program with CSS

Programming with CSS (Cascading Style Sheets) involves writing code to define the presentation, layout, and styling of web documents, typically HTML documents. CSS is used to control the visual appearance of web pages, including fonts, colors, spacing, and positioning. Here's a step-by-step guide on how to program with CSS:

Create an HTML Document:

- Before you can apply CSS styling, you need an HTML document to work with. Create an HTML file (e.g., index.html) using a text editor or an integrated development environment (IDE).

Link CSS Stylesheet:

- In the <head> section of your HTML document, link an external CSS stylesheet using the <link> element. For example:

```
<!DOCTYPE html>
```

```html
<html>
<head>
    <link rel="stylesheet"
type="text/css"
href="styles.css">
    <title>My Web Page</title>
</head>
<body>
    <!-- Content goes here -->
</body>
</html>
```

In this example, the CSS stylesheet is named styles.css. You can also include CSS directly in the HTML document using the <style> element.

Create a CSS File:

- Create a CSS file (e.g., styles.css) in the same directory as your HTML file. This is where you'll write your CSS rules.

Write CSS Rules:

- CSS rules consist of selectors, properties, and values. Selectors target HTML elements, properties define the styling, and values set the style's attributes. Here's an example CSS rule:

```css
/* CSS comment */
h1 {
    color: blue;
    font-size: 24px;
    text-align: center;
}
```

- In this example, the selector h1 targets all <h1> elements in the HTML document. The properties color, font-size, and text-align set the color, font size, and text alignment of those elements.

Apply CSS Styling:

- To apply CSS styling, add HTML elements in your document and assign CSS classes or IDs to them as needed. For example:

```html
<h1>This is a Heading</h1>
```

```
<p class="highlighted">This is a
paragraph with custom
styling.</p>
```

- In this example, the <h1> element is styled according to the h1 CSS rule, while the <p> element has a custom class highlighted applied to it.

Test Your Web Page:

- Open your HTML document in a web browser to view the styled web page. Any CSS rules you've defined in the linked stylesheet or <style> element will be applied to the HTML elements.

Inspect and Debug:

- Use the browser's built-in developer tools to inspect and debug your CSS styles. You can make real-time adjustments to the styles and see the changes in your web page.

Learn CSS Properties:

- CSS offers a wide range of properties and values for styling. Familiarize yourself with common properties like color, font-size, margin, padding, background, and more. Explore CSS documentation and tutorials to learn about advanced properties and features.

Practice and Experiment:

- Experiment with different CSS selectors, properties, and values to achieve the desired styling effects. Practice by creating various layouts and designs.

Responsive Design (Advanced):

- Learn about responsive design principles and techniques to make your web pages look good on different devices and screen sizes. CSS media queries are essential for responsive design.

CSS Preprocessors (Optional):

- Consider learning CSS preprocessors like Sass or Less, which offer additional features and enhance the organization of your stylesheets.

CSS Frameworks (Optional):

- Explore popular CSS frameworks like Bootstrap or Foundation to leverage pre-designed UI components and responsive layouts for your web projects.

By following these steps and continuously experimenting with CSS, you can become proficient in styling and designing web pages to create visually appealing and responsive websites.

Programming with LaTeX

Programming with LaTeX involves using LaTeX, a typesetting system commonly used for creating documents with complex formatting, mathematical content, and academic papers. LaTeX uses markup commands to define the structure and appearance of documents. Here's a step-by-step guide on how to program with LaTeX:

Install LaTeX Distribution:
First, you need to install a LaTeX distribution on your computer. Popular distributions include TeX Live (cross-platform), MiKTeX (Windows), and MacTeX (macOS). Choose the one that suits your operating system and install it.
Choose an Editor:
LaTeX files are plain text files, so you can use any text editor to write LaTeX code. However, specialized LaTeX editors provide features like syntax highlighting, autocompletion, and built-in PDF preview. Some popular LaTeX editors include TeXShop (macOS), TeXworks (cross-platform), and TeXstudio (cross-platform).

Alternatively, you can use LaTeX extensions in Visual Studio Code or Atom.

Create a LaTeX Document:

Create a new LaTeX document with a .tex file extension using your chosen text editor. A basic LaTeX document structure includes:

```
\documentclass{article}
\begin{document}
% Your content goes here
\end{document}
```

- `\documentclass{article}`: Specifies the type of document you are creating (e.g., article, book, report).
- `\begin{document}` and `\end{document}`: Define the beginning and end of the document content.

Add Content:

```
Write your document content
within the \begin{document}
```

```
and \end{document} tags.
LaTeX provides a wide range
of commands for structuring
text, creating sections,
formatting text, and more.
For example:
```

`\section{Introduction}`

This is the introduction to my document. LaTeX provides powerful typesetting features for formatting text, equations, and more.

`\subsection{Subsection}`

Here's a subsection.

- `\section{}`: Creates a section heading.
- `\subsection{}`: Creates a subsection heading.

Compile the Document:
To generate a PDF document from your LaTeX source code, you need to compile it. Use your LaTeX editor's built-in compiler or open a

terminal/command prompt and navigate to the directory containing your .tex file. Run the following commands:

```
pdflatex your-document.tex
```

This command will produce a PDF file called your-document.pdf.

View the PDF:

Open the generated PDF document in a PDF viewer to see the formatted output. LaTeX will automatically format and paginate your document based on the commands and packages you used in your .tex file.

Learn LaTeX Commands:

LaTeX offers a wide range of commands for formatting text, creating lists, tables, equations, and more. Familiarize yourself with common LaTeX commands by referring to LaTeX documentation and tutorials.

Use Packages:

LaTeX packages extend its

functionality for specific purposes. For example, you can use the amsmath package for advanced math formatting or the graphicx package for including images. Include packages using the `\usepackage{package-name}` command in the preamble (before `\begin{document}`).

Advanced Topics:

LaTeX supports more advanced features like creating bibliographies, customizing page layouts, and using templates. Explore these topics as needed for your projects.

Templates and Customization:

To speed up document creation, you can use LaTeX templates that provide pre-defined structures and formatting for various document types. Customize templates to suit your needs.

Collaboration and Version Control:

If collaborating on LaTeX documents, consider using version control systems like Git. Collaborators can work on the same document simultaneously, and Git helps track changes and revisions. Resources: Refer to LaTeX documentation, books, and online tutorials to enhance your LaTeX skills. LaTeX has a rich and supportive user community.

Programming with LaTeX allows you to create professional-quality documents with precise formatting and mathematical notation. With practice and exploration, you can become proficient in using LaTeX for various types of documents, including research papers, theses, reports, and more.

Programming with Gherkin

Programming with Gherkin involves writing Gherkin scenarios and feature files to define behavior-driven development (BDD) tests. Gherkin is a domain-specific language used in conjunction with BDD frameworks like Cucumber and Behave. It focuses on describing the behavior of software in plain text. Here's a step-by-step guide on how to program with Gherkin:

Choose a BDD Framework:

- Gherkin is often used with BDD frameworks like Cucumber (for Java, Ruby, and other languages), Behave (for Python), SpecFlow (for .NET), and more. Choose a framework that aligns with your programming language and project requirements.

Set Up Your Development Environment:

- Install the chosen BDD framework and any required dependencies for your programming language. You'll also need a code editor or integrated development environment (IDE).

Create a Feature File:

- In BDD, you start by creating a
  .feature file. This file typically
  resides in a dedicated "features"
  directory within your project.
  Feature files use the Gherkin
  language to define behavior
  scenarios for specific features of
  your application.

Define a Feature:

- Begin your .feature file by
  defining the feature you want to
  describe. Use the Feature:
  keyword followed by a
  descriptive title. For example:

Feature: Login Functionality
 As a user,
 I want to be able to log in to my account
 So that I can access my personalized
content.

Write Scenarios:

- Scenarios describe specific
  behaviors or test cases for the
  feature. Use the Scenario:

keyword followed by a scenario title. Each scenario should be a concrete example of how the feature should work. For example:

Scenario: Successful Login
  Given the user is on the login page
  When the user enters valid credentials
  Then the user should be logged in
  And they should see their dashboard.

- Use keywords like Given, When, Then, and And to describe the steps that lead to the desired behavior.

Write Scenario Steps:

- Define each step of the scenario in Gherkin. The steps map to automated test code that interacts with your application. For example:

```
Given the user is on the login
page
```

```gherkin
When the user enters valid
credentials
Then the user should be logged
in
And they should see their
dashboard.
```

Implement Step Definitions:

- Gherkin steps must be linked to actual code that performs the actions described in the steps. This code is written in your programming language of choice. Each step corresponds to a step definition. For example, in Java with Cucumber, a step definition might look like this:

```java
@Given("the user is on the login
page")
public void
the_user_is_on_the_login_page()
{
    // Implementation code to
navigate to the login page
```

}

- Create step definition files to implement the behavior for each step in your scenarios.

Run Tests:

- Use the BDD framework's command-line interface or a test runner to execute your Gherkin-based tests. This will trigger the automation of the steps defined in your scenarios.

Review Test Results:

- After running the tests, review the test results to check if your application behaves as expected. The test results should indicate whether each scenario passed or failed.

Iterate and Maintain:

- As you develop your application, you may need to modify or add new scenarios. Update the feature files and step definitions accordingly. Continuously maintain and improve your Gherkin scenarios and automated tests as the application evolves.

Collaborate with Stakeholders:

- Gherkin scenarios are often written in collaboration with stakeholders, including product managers, developers, and testers. They provide a common language for discussing and specifying software behavior.

Learn Gherkin Syntax and Best Practices:

- Study Gherkin's syntax and best practices to write clear, concise, and maintainable scenarios. Avoid duplication and aim for a descriptive and readable style.

Programming with Gherkin allows you to create executable specifications that serve as documentation, tests, and collaboration tools. It promotes communication between technical and non-technical team members and helps ensure that software behavior aligns with business requirements.

Programming with MDX

Programming with MDX (Multidimensional Expressions) involves writing queries and expressions to work with multidimensional data models, particularly in the context of OLAP (Online Analytical Processing) systems and databases. MDX is used for retrieving and manipulating data from cubes and hierarchies in a multidimensional database. Here's a step-by-step guide on how to program with MDX:

Understand Multidimensional Data: Before working with MDX, it's essential to understand the concept of multidimensional data. Multidimensional data is organized into cubes, which consist of dimensions and measures. Dimensions represent attributes or

hierarchies, while measures represent numerical values you want to analyze.
Choose an OLAP System:
MDX is primarily used with OLAP databases and systems like Microsoft Analysis Services, SAP BW, and Mondrian. Choose an OLAP system that aligns with your project's requirements and install/configure it.
Connect to the OLAP Database:
Use a client tool or query interface to connect to your OLAP database. Most OLAP systems provide management tools and query interfaces where you can write and execute MDX queries.
Learn MDX Syntax:
MDX queries and expressions have a specific syntax. Familiarize yourself with MDX keywords, functions, and operators. MDX queries are similar in structure to SQL queries but are tailored for multidimensional data.
Write Basic MDX Queries:
Start by writing basic MDX queries to

retrieve data from cubes. Here's a simple example:

```
SELECT [Measures].[Sales] ON
COLUMNS,
        [Time].[Year].Members ON
ROWS
FROM [SalesCube]
```

- This query retrieves sales data over different years.

Understand MDX Functions:
MDX includes numerous functions for performing calculations and aggregations. For example, the SUM, COUNT, and FILTER functions allow you to manipulate and aggregate data.
Specify Dimensions and Hierarchies:
In MDX, you specify dimensions and hierarchies to retrieve data at different levels of granularity. For instance:

```
SELECT [Measures].[Profit] ON
COLUMNS,
```

```
[Product].[Category].[Category].
Members ON ROWS
FROM [SalesCube]
```

- This query retrieves profit data for each product category.

Filter and Sort Data:
Use MDX to filter and sort data as needed for your analysis. You can use functions like FILTER and ORDER to achieve this.

Learn About Named Sets:
MDX allows you to create named sets, which are reusable subsets of data. Named sets can simplify complex queries and calculations.

Master MDX Calculations:
MDX supports custom calculations, including calculated members and named calculations. You can use these to create calculated measures and members based on existing data.

Practice with Sample Data:
If your OLAP system provides sample data or demo cubes, use them to practice writing MDX queries and exploring the multidimensional model.

Debug and Optimize Queries:
Debug MDX queries by analyzing query execution plans and optimizing them for better performance. Understanding the query execution process is crucial for optimization.

Use MDX in Reports and Dashboards: Integrate MDX queries into reporting tools and dashboards to visualize multidimensional data. Many reporting tools support MDX queries for OLAP data sources.

Refer to MDX Documentation: MDX can be quite powerful and complex. Refer to MDX documentation specific to your OLAP system for detailed information on functions, syntax, and best practices.

Programming with MDX is essential for business intelligence, data analysis, and reporting in scenarios where multidimensional data models are used. With practice and a solid understanding of multidimensional data, you can write effective MDX queries and leverage OLAP systems to gain valuable insights from your data.

Programming with PromQL

Programming with PromQL (Prometheus Query Language) involves writing queries to retrieve and analyze time-series data collected and stored by Prometheus, an open-source monitoring and alerting toolkit. PromQL allows you to query and manipulate these time-series metrics to gain insights into the performance and health of your systems. Here's a step-by-step guide on how to program with PromQL:

Set Up Prometheus:

To work with PromQL, you need a

running Prometheus server collecting and storing time-series data. Install Prometheus, configure it to scrape metrics from your target services, and ensure that it's up and running.

Access Prometheus Web UI:

Prometheus comes with a web-based user interface that allows you to write and test PromQL queries interactively. Access the Prometheus web UI by navigating to http://your-prometheus-instance:9090/ in your web browser.

Learn PromQL Basics:

Familiarize yourself with the basics of PromQL, including metric names, labels, and the fundamental concepts of time-series data. PromQL is specifically designed for querying this type of data.

Use the Web UI:

In the Prometheus web UI, go to the "Graph" tab. Here, you can write and execute PromQL queries. Enter a query in the text box and click "Execute" to visualize the results as graphs.

Retrieve Metrics:

Start with simple queries to retrieve metrics. For example, to retrieve the CPU usage metric for a target named my_app, use the cpu_usage metric name and the instance label:

```
cpu_usage{instance="my_app"}
```

This query selects all time series that match the specified criteria.

Filter by Time Range:

You can filter metrics by specifying a time range using the timestamp operator. For example, to retrieve the last 5 minutes of CPU usage data:

```
cpu_usage{instance="my_app",
timestamp > now() - 5m}
```

Aggregate Data:

PromQL allows you to perform aggregations on time series data. Common aggregation functions include sum(), avg(), max(), and min(). For example, to calculate the average CPU usage for all instances:

```
avg(cpu_usage)
```

Group and Filter Data:
You can group and filter data using the by clause. For instance, to calculate the maximum CPU usage per instance:

```
max(cpu_usage) by (instance)
```

Perform Mathematical Operations:
PromQL supports mathematical operations on time series data. You can perform operations like addition, subtraction, and multiplication between time series. For example, to calculate the difference in CPU usage between two instances:

```
cpu_usage{instance="instance_a"}
-
cpu_usage{instance="instance_b"}
```

Use Functions and Operators:
PromQL provides a variety of
functions and operators for
manipulating and transforming data.
Explore functions like rate(), irate(),
changes(), and operators like ==, =~,
and !=.
Alerting Rules:
In addition to querying, Prometheus
uses PromQL in alerting rules to
define alert conditions. Write alerting
rules that trigger alerts based on
specific criteria and thresholds.
Integration with Grafana:
Grafana is a popular visualization tool
that integrates with Prometheus. You
can use Grafana to create dashboards
that visualize PromQL queries and
make them more accessible.
Practice and Experiment:
Practice writing PromQL queries with
various scenarios and data types.
Experiment with different functions

and operators to understand how they affect query results.
Documentation and Resources:
Refer to Prometheus and PromQL documentation for in-depth guidance and best practices. The Prometheus website and community forums are valuable resources for learning and troubleshooting.
Programming with PromQL is crucial for monitoring and alerting in a modern IT environment. With proficiency in PromQL, you can effectively query and analyze time-series data to monitor the health and performance of your systems and applications.

Programming with YAML

Programming with YAML (YAML Ain't Markup Language) involves writing structured data in a human-readable format. YAML is often used for configuration files, data serialization, and other scenarios where data needs to be stored in a plain text format. Here's a step-by-step guide on how to program with YAML:

Understand YAML Basics:
- YAML is a text-based data format that uses indentation to represent hierarchical structure.
- It is designed to be easy for humans to read and write, making it a popular choice for configuration files.

Choose a YAML Editor:
- YAML files are plain text files, so you can use any text editor to create and edit them. However, using a code editor or an IDE with YAML support can provide syntax highlighting and validation, which can help prevent errors.

Learn YAML Syntax:
- YAML uses a straightforward syntax that includes key-value

pairs, lists, and nested structures.

- YAML documents start with three dashes (---) to indicate the beginning of a document.
- Key-value pairs are written with a colon (:) separating the key and the value.
- Lists are represented with a hyphen (-) followed by the list item.
- Comments start with the # symbol.

Create YAML Files:

- Create a new YAML file with a .yaml or .yml file extension using your chosen text editor.

Write Key-Value Pairs:

- Use key-value pairs to store data in your YAML file. For example:

```yaml
name: John Doe
age: 30
email: johndoe@example.com
```

Work with Lists:

- Lists in YAML are represented as follows:

```
fruits:
  - apple
  - banana
  - orange
```

- You can have nested lists as well:

```
countries:
 - name: USA
   capital: Washington, D.C.
  - name: Canada
   capital: Ottawa
```

Indentation:

- YAML relies on indentation for structure. Be consistent with the number of spaces or tabs you use for indentation. Common practice is to use two spaces for indentation.

Comments:

- Add comments to your YAML files using the # symbol. Comments are for documentation and are ignored during parsing.

```
# This is a comment
name: John Doe
```

Scalar Types:

- YAML supports various scalar data types, including strings, numbers, booleans, and null values.

```
string: "This is a string"
number: 42
boolean: true
null_value: null
```

Learn About YAML Anchors and Aliases (Advanced):

- YAML allows you to reuse the same data across your file using anchors and aliases. This is

useful for avoiding duplication
in your YAML documents.

```
first_name: &name John
last_name: &name Doe

full_name: *name
```

Use YAML in Configuration Files:
- YAML is commonly used for configuration files in various software projects. Study the documentation for the software you're working with to understand how it uses YAML for configuration.

Validation and Linting:
- Consider using YAML validation tools or linters to check your YAML files for syntax errors and adherence to best practices.

Documentation and Resources:
- Refer to the official YAML specification and YAML-related documentation for more

in-depth information on YAML syntax and features. Programming with YAML is straightforward, and it's widely used for various tasks in software development and configuration management. Whether you're writing configuration files for an application or storing structured data in a human-readable format, YAML is a versatile choice.

Programming with Regular Expressions

Programming with regular expressions (regex or regexp) involves using a powerful pattern-matching language to search, match, and manipulate text strings based on specific patterns. Regular expressions are commonly used in text processing tasks, data validation, and search operations. Here's a step-by-step guide on how to program with regular expressions:

Choose a Programming Language:
Regular expressions are supported in many programming languages, including Python, JavaScript, Java, C#, PHP, and more. Choose a language that suits your project and is familiar to you.

Learn Basic Syntax:
Start by understanding the basic syntax of regular expressions:

- Literals: Characters like letters and digits match themselves. For example, the regex abc matches the string "abc" exactly.
- Metacharacters: Special characters like ., *, +, ?, [,], (,), {, }, |, \, and ^ have special meanings in regex. For example, . matches any character except a newline, * matches zero or more of the preceding character, and [...] defines a character class.

Select a Regex Tester:
To experiment with regular expressions, use an online regex tester or an integrated development environment (IDE) with regex support. These tools allow you to write regex patterns and test them against sample text.
Define Your Problem:
Clearly define the problem you want to solve with regular expressions. Identify the specific patterns you need to match or extract from text.
Write a Regex Pattern:
Write a regex pattern that describes the desired pattern or text you want to match. Be as specific as possible. Use metacharacters, character classes, and quantifiers as needed.
Test Your Pattern:
Test your regex pattern using a regex tester. Input sample text that contains instances of the pattern you want to match. Verify that your pattern

correctly identifies and captures the desired text.

Understand Groups and Capturing: Regular expressions allow you to group parts of a pattern and capture them. Use parentheses () to create groups, and the matched text within parentheses can be extracted separately.

For example, in the pattern `(\d{2})-(\d{2})-(\d{4})`, there are three groups for day, month, and year.

Practice Escaping Special Characters: When you want to match a literal metacharacter, you need to escape it with a backslash \. For example, to match a literal period (.), you would write \..

Use Anchors:

Anchors like ^ (start of a line) and $ (end of a line) allow you to specify where in the text the pattern should match. For example, ^start will only match if "start" appears at the beginning of a line.

Modifiers and Flags:

Many regex engines support modifiers or flags that modify how the pattern is matched. Common flags include i for case-insensitive matching and g for global matching.

Replace and Manipulate Text:

Regular expressions can be used for text manipulation tasks. In many programming languages, you can use functions like replace() to replace matched text with other text or patterns.

Learn About Lookaheads and Lookbehinds (Advanced):

Lookaheads ((?=...)) and lookbehinds ((?<=...)) are advanced features that allow you to match patterns based on what comes before or after without consuming those characters.

Learn Regular Expression Libraries:

Study the documentation for the regex

library in your chosen programming
language to understand the specific
functions and methods available for
regex processing.
Optimize and Simplify:
Regular expressions can become
complex. Always aim to write patterns
that are as simple and efficient as
possible to avoid performance issues.
Practice and Experiment:
Regular expressions can be
challenging, so practice is essential.
Experiment with different patterns
and test them against various inputs
to gain confidence and expertise.
Resources and Documentation:
Refer to the official documentation for
regular expressions in your
programming language to learn more
about syntax, functions, and advanced
features.
Programming with regular expressions can
be a powerful tool for text processing and
pattern matching tasks. With practice and a

good understanding of the regex syntax, you can efficiently solve a wide range of text-related problems.

Markup Languages

What is a Markup Language? A markup language is a system for annotating text or data with additional information, known as "markup." This additional information defines the structure, formatting, and semantics of the content. Markup languages use tags, elements, or annotations to achieve this.

Key Characteristics of Markup Languages:

Tags or Elements: Markup languages use tags or elements to enclose and define different parts of the content. Tags are often enclosed in angle brackets (< >).

Attributes: Elements can have attributes that provide additional

information about the element or modify its behavior.
Nested Structure: Elements can be nested inside other elements to represent hierarchical relationships.
Semantic Meaning: Markup languages often convey semantic meaning, helping computers and humans understand the content's structure and purpose.

Common Markup Languages:
HTML (Hypertext Markup Language): HTML is the standard markup language for creating web pages. It defines the structure and content of web documents using elements like <html>, <head>, <body>, and many others.
XML (eXtensible Markup Language): XML is a versatile markup language used for data representation and interchange. It allows users to define their custom tags and structures,

making it highly adaptable to various domains.

Markdown: Markdown is a lightweight markup language used for formatting plain text. It's commonly used for writing documents, readme files, and online content.

LaTeX: LaTeX is a markup language often used for typesetting documents, particularly in academic and scientific writing. It provides fine-grained control over document formatting.

YAML (YAML Ain't Markup Language): YAML is a human-readable data serialization format that uses indentation and simple syntax. It's used for configuration files, data storage, and more.

Use Cases for Markup Languages:

Web Development: HTML is used to create web pages, defining their structure, content, and presentation.

Data Representation: XML and JSON are used for data interchange between systems and for representing structured data.

Document Creation: LaTeX is popular for creating high-quality documents, such as research papers, theses, and scientific publications.

Configuration Files: Markup languages like YAML are used for configuring software applications.

Content Management: Markdown is often used for creating content in content management systems (CMS) and for writing documentation.

Benefits of Markup Languages:

Structure: Markup languages provide a clear and structured way to represent content, making it easier for both humans and computers to interpret.

Portability: Markup files are typically plain text, making them platform-independent and easy to share.

Customization: Many markup languages allow users to define their custom elements and attributes, providing flexibility.

Interoperability: Markup languages facilitate data exchange and interoperability between different software systems.

Challenges:

Syntax Sensitivity: Markup languages can be sensitive to syntax errors, which may lead to rendering or processing issues.

Learning Curve: Learning the syntax and rules of markup languages can be challenging for beginners.

Complexity: Some markup languages, like XML, can become complex for large and highly structured documents.

Data science is a multidisciplinary field that involves extracting knowledge and insights from data through various techniques, including statistical analysis, machine learning, data mining, and data visualization. Statistical programming languages are critical tools in the data science toolkit. Here's everything you need to know about data science and statistical languages:

Programming with XML

Programming with XML (eXtensible Markup Language) involves working with structured data represented in a hierarchical format using XML tags. XML is commonly used for data interchange and storage. Here's a step-by-step guide on how to program with XML:

1. Understanding XML:
   - XML is a markup language that uses tags to define elements and their structure.

- Each XML document has a root element that contains nested elements.

2. Create an XML Document:

- To create an XML document, you can use a text editor or an XML-specific editor or IDE. XML documents typically have the .xml file extension.

```xml
<?xml version="1.0" encoding="UTF-8"?>
<bookstore>
    <book>
        <title>Introduction to XML</title>
        <author>John Doe</author>
        <price>29.95</price>
    </book>
    <book>
        <title>XML Programming Basics</title>
        <author>Jane Smith</author>
        <price>39.95</price>
```

```
</book>
```
</bookstore>

3. XML Tags:
- XML elements are enclosed in tags. Tags are case-sensitive and should be properly nested.
- Opening tag: <element>
- Closing tag: </element>

4. XML Attributes:
- XML elements can have attributes that provide additional information. Attributes are specified within the opening tag.

```
<book id="1">
    <title>Introduction to
XML</title>
    <author>John Doe</author>
    <price
currency="USD">29.95</price>
</book>
```

5. XML Document Declaration:

- An XML document typically starts
  with a declaration that specifies the
  version of XML being used and the
  character encoding.

`<?xml version="1.0" encoding="UTF-8"?>`

6. XML Validation:
   - You can validate XML documents
     against a Document Type Definition
     (DTD) or an XML Schema Definition
     (XSD) to enforce data structure and
     format rules.
7. Parsing XML:
   - To work with XML data
     programmatically, you need to parse it
     using a programming language. Most
     languages have libraries or modules
     for XML parsing.
8. Using XML Libraries:
   - Depending on the programming
     language, you may use libraries or
     built-in modules to parse and
     manipulate XML data. Common
     choices include:

- Python: xml.etree.ElementTree
  or third-party libraries like lxml.
- Java: Java provides built-in
  libraries like javax.xml.parsers
  for XML parsing.
- C#: .NET includes System.Xml
  for working with XML.
- JavaScript: The browser's DOM
  (Document Object Model) can
  be used for parsing XML in web
  applications.

9. Reading XML Data:
- Use the XML parsing library to read
  XML data into memory, typically as a
  data structure that represents the
  document's structure.

10. Navigating and Modifying Data:
- Traverse the XML data structure to access,
modify, or extract specific elements or
attributes.

11. Writing XML Data:

- Generate or modify XML data in memory, and then use the library to write it back to a file or send it as output.

12. XPath and XQuery (Optional):
- XPath and XQuery are query languages for XML data that allow you to retrieve specific data from XML documents based on patterns and conditions.

13. XML Transformation (Optional):
- XSLT (eXtensible Stylesheet Language Transformations) can be used to transform XML documents into different formats, such as HTML or another XML structure.

14. Best Practices:
- Follow XML best practices, such as proper indentation, meaningful element and attribute names, and consistent coding standards.

15. Error Handling:

- Implement error handling to deal with issues such as malformed XML documents or missing data.

16. Security Considerations:
- Be aware of security concerns when processing XML, such as XML injection vulnerabilities.

17. Testing and Validation:

- Validate XML documents to ensure they adhere to the specified schema or DTD.

18. Documentation and Resources:
- Refer to language-specific documentation and resources for XML programming in your chosen programming language.

19. Real-World Applications:
- Apply XML programming in real-world scenarios, such as data interchange, configuration files, web services, and more.

XML programming is a fundamental skill for working with structured data in many domains, including web development, data exchange, configuration management, and data storage. Whether you're building web services, processing configuration files, or working with data feeds, XML is a versatile format that plays a crucial role in modern computing.

Programming with Markdown

Programming with Markdown involves creating and formatting plain text documents using Markdown syntax. Markdown is a lightweight markup language that is easy to learn and widely used for writing documentation, creating README files, and formatting content for the web. Here's a step-by-step guide on how to program with Markdown:

1. Text Editor:
   - You can create Markdown documents using a simple text editor like Notepad

(on Windows), TextEdit (on macOS), or any code editor such as Visual Studio Code, Sublime Text, or Atom.

2. Basic Markdown Syntax:
   - Markdown uses simple and intuitive syntax. Here are some basic elements:
     - Headers: Use # to create headings (1 to 6 # characters for different levels).
     - Lists: Create ordered (numbered) and unordered (bulleted) lists using -, +, or * for unordered and numbers for ordered lists.
     - Emphasis: Use * or _ for italics and ** or __ for bold.
     - Links: Create links using [text](URL).
     - Images: Insert images using `![alt text](image URL)`.
     - Code: Inline code can be enclosed in backticks (\``) like inline code`, and code blocks can be created by indenting with

four spaces or using triple backticks (```).

3. Headers:
   - Create headers using # (H1), ## (H2), and so on up to ###### (H6).

```
# This is a Header 1
## This is a Header 2
### This is a Header 3
```

4. Lists:
   - Create lists by using -, +, or * for unordered lists and numbers for ordered lists.

```
- Item 1
- Item 2
- Item 3
```

```
1. First item
2. Second item
3. Third item
```

5. Emphasis:
   - Use * or _ to create italics and ** or ___ for bold.

```
*Italic Text*
_Italic Text_
**Bold Text**
__Bold Text__
```

6. Links and Images:
   - Create links using [text](URL) and insert images using `![alt text](image URL)`.

[Visit Google](https://www.google.com)
`![Logo](https://example.com/logo.png)`

7. Code:
   - Inline code can be enclosed in backticks, and code blocks can be created by indenting with four spaces or using triple backticks (```) for fenced code blocks.

Inline code: `code here`

Code Block

8. Quotes:

- Create blockquotes using `>`.

```markdown
> This is a blockquote.
```

9. Horizontal Lines:
   - Create horizontal lines using ---, ***,
     or ____.
---

10. Tables:
- Create tables using pipe `|` characters to
separate columns.

```markdown
| Header 1 | Header 2 |
| --------- | --------- |
| Row 1, Col 1 | Row 1, Col 2 |
| Row 2, Col 1 | Row 2, Col 2 |
```

11. HTML:

- Markdown also allows you to use HTML tags for more complex formatting if needed.

```markdown
<div style="background-color: lightgray;">This is a gray box.</div>
```


12. Preview and Render:
- Many text editors and Markdown editors provide live previews of Markdown documents, making it easier to see the formatted output as you write.

13. Export and Share:
- Once you've written and formatted your Markdown document, you can save it with the `.md` extension and share it as needed. GitHub, GitLab, and many content management systems (like WordPress) support Markdown formatting.

Markdown is a simple and versatile markup language that is particularly useful for creating documentation, blog posts, README files for software projects, and more. It provides a lightweight and easy-to-read format that can be easily converted into HTML or other formats when needed.

Data Science and Statistical Languages

What is Data Science?

Data science is the practice of collecting, processing, analyzing, and interpreting large volumes of data to extract valuable insights, inform decision-making, and solve complex problems. Data scientists use a combination of domain knowledge, statistical methods, programming skills, and data manipulation tools to uncover hidden patterns and trends in data.

Key Steps in Data Science:

Data Collection: Gathering data from various sources, which may include databases, APIs, sensors, and more.
Data Cleaning and Preprocessing: Cleaning, transforming, and structuring data to ensure its quality and suitability for analysis.
Exploratory Data Analysis (EDA): Exploring and visualizing data to understand its characteristics and identify potential patterns.
Feature Engineering: Selecting, creating, or transforming relevant features (variables) for modeling.
Statistical Analysis: Applying statistical methods to gain insights, test hypotheses, and make predictions from the data.
Machine Learning: Developing and training machine learning models for classification, regression, clustering, and other tasks.

Data Visualization: Creating informative visualizations to communicate findings effectively.
Model Evaluation: Assessing model performance using metrics and validation techniques.
Deployment: Integrating data science solutions into applications or systems for practical use.

Statistical Languages in Data Science:
Statistical programming languages are essential for data manipulation, analysis, and modeling in data science. Some of the popular statistical languages include:

R: R is a specialized language and environment for statistical computing and graphics. It has a rich ecosystem of packages for data manipulation, visualization, and statistical analysis.

Python: Python is a versatile programming language with libraries like NumPy, Pandas, SciPy, Matplotlib, and scikit-learn that provide powerful tools for data science, machine learning, and scientific computing.

Julia: Julia is a high-level, high-performance language for technical computing, including data analysis and scientific computing. It's known for its speed and ease of use in numerical and statistical tasks.

SAS: SAS (Statistical Analysis System) is a software suite commonly used in the industry for data analytics, advanced analytics, and statistical modeling.

Key Concepts in Statistical Languages:

Data Structures: Statistical languages provide data structures like vectors, matrices, data frames, and lists to store and manipulate data.

Data Manipulation: Functions and libraries allow users to perform data cleaning, transformation, aggregation, and merging operations.

Statistical Analysis: Built-in functions and packages provide tools for hypothesis testing, regression analysis, correlation, and more.
Visualization: Libraries offer various options for creating static and interactive data visualizations to communicate insights effectively.
Machine Learning: Statistical languages integrate machine learning libraries and frameworks for tasks like classification, regression, clustering, and deep learning.
Packages and Libraries: The power of statistical languages lies in their extensive packages and libraries that extend their capabilities in specific domains.

Challenges in Data Science:

Data Quality: Ensuring the accuracy, completeness, and reliability of data can be challenging.

Data Volume: Handling large datasets may require specialized techniques and infrastructure.

Model Interpretability: Understanding complex machine learning models and explaining their decisions can be difficult.

Ethical Considerations: Data scientists must consider ethical implications when working with data, including privacy and bias issues.

Continuous Learning: Data science is a rapidly evolving field, requiring practitioners to stay updated with the latest techniques and tools.

Applications of Data Science:

Data science is applied in various industries and domains, including finance, healthcare, e-commerce, marketing, cybersecurity, and more. Some common applications include fraud detection, predictive maintenance, recommendation systems, and medical diagnosis.

In conclusion, data science is a dynamic field that leverages statistical languages and techniques to extract valuable insights from data. It plays a critical role in decision-making and problem-solving across a wide range of industries and domains. To excel in data science, practitioners need a combination of technical skills, domain expertise, and a solid understanding of statistical concepts and programming languages.

Programming with Julia

Programming with Julia involves writing code in the Julia programming language, which is known for its high-performance, scientific computing capabilities, and ease of use. Here's a step-by-step guide on how to program with Julia:

1. Install Julia:

   - Download the Julia programming language from the official website (https://julialang.org/downloads/).

- Follow the installation instructions for your specific operating system.

2. Julia REPL (Read-Eval-Print Loop):
   - Launch the Julia REPL by running the julia command in your terminal or command prompt.

3. Basic Julia Syntax:
   - Julia has a familiar syntax similar to Python and other programming languages. You can start by writing basic expressions and statements in the REPL.

```julia
# Hello World
println("Hello, Julia!")
```

   - Julia supports common programming constructs like variables, loops, conditionals, and functions.

4. Variables and Data Types:
   - Declare variables and specify data types. Julia offers a range of numeric types (Int, Float), strings, and more.

```julia
x = 5
y = "Julia"
```

5. Control Structures:
- Use if-else statements for conditional execution:

```julia
if x > 0
    println("x is positive")
else
    println("x is non-positive")
end
```

- Create loops using for and while constructs:

```julia
for i in 1:5
    println("Iteration $i")
end
```

6. Functions:
- Define functions in Julia using the function keyword:

```julia
function greet(name)
  println("Hello, $name!")
end
```

- Call functions with arguments:

```julia
greet("Alice")
```

7. Packages and Modules:
   - Julia has a rich ecosystem of packages
     for various purposes. You can use the
     Julia package manager to install and
     manage packages.

```julia
using Pkg
Pkg.add("Plots")
```

   - Import modules and use functions
     from packages in your code.
8. Data Manipulation:
   - Julia has built-in support for data
     manipulation with arrays,
     dictionaries, and other data
     structures.

```julia
# Create an array
numbers = [1, 2, 3, 4, 5]

# Perform operations on the array
total = sum(numbers)
```

9. Plotting and Visualization:

- Julia offers packages like Plots.jl for creating visualizations and plots.

```julia
using Plots
x = 1:0.1:10
y = sin.(x)
plot(x, y)
```

10. Advanced Topics:
    - As you become more proficient with Julia, explore advanced topics such as metaprogramming, parallel computing, and GPU programming.
11. Documentation and Resources:
    - Refer to the official Julia documentation (https://docs.julialang.org/) and community resources for learning and troubleshooting.
12. IDEs and Editors:
    - Consider using integrated development environments (IDEs) or text editors with Julia support, such as JuliaPro, Juno, or Visual Studio Code with the Julia extension.

13. Practice and Projects:
- Learning by doing is crucial in programming. Work on projects, solve problems, and practice coding regularly to improve your Julia skills.

Julia is a versatile and powerful language, particularly suited for numerical and scientific computing tasks. Whether you're working on data analysis, machine learning, or scientific simulations, Julia can be a valuable addition to your programming toolkit.

Programming with R

Programming with R involves using the R programming language, which is specifically designed for data analysis and statistical computing. R is known for its rich ecosystem of statistical and graphical packages. Here's a step-by-step guide on how to program with R:

1. Install R:

- Download the R software from the Comprehensive R Archive Network (CRAN) website (https://cran.r-project.org/).
- Follow the installation instructions for your specific operating system.

2. R Console:

- Launch the R console by running the R command in your terminal or command prompt.

3. Basic R Syntax:

- R uses a simple and expressive syntax for data analysis. You can start by entering basic expressions and statements in the R console.

```
# Hello World
print("Hello, R!")
```

- R supports variables, data types, and basic operations like arithmetic and logical operations.

4. Variables and Data Types:

- Declare variables and specify data
  types. R provides data types such as
  numeric, character, logical, and more.

```
x <- 5
y <- "R"
```

5. Control Structures:
    - Use if-else statements for conditional
      execution:

```
if (x > 0) {
  print("x is positive")
} else {
  print("x is non-positive")
}
```

    - Create loops using for and while
      constructs:

```
for (i in 1:5) {
    print(paste("Iteration", i))
}
```

6. Functions:
    - Define functions in R using the
      function keyword:

```r
greet <- function(name) {
    print(paste("Hello,", name,
"!"))
}
```

- Call functions with arguments: greet("Alice")

7. Packages and Libraries:
  - R has a vast repository of packages and libraries that extend its functionality. You can install and manage packages using the install.packages() and library() functions.

```r
install.packages("ggplot2")
library(ggplot2)
```

8. Data Manipulation:
  - R excels in data manipulation with features like data frames, which are used to store and manipulate tabular data.

```r
# Create a data frame
```

```r
data <- data.frame(ID = 1:5,
Name = c("Alice", "Bob",
"Charlie", "David", "Eve"))
```

- R provides functions like subset(), filter(), mutate(), and group_by() for data manipulation.

9. Data Visualization:
   - R is known for its excellent data visualization capabilities. Libraries like ggplot2 are popular for creating rich and customized plots.

```r
# Create a scatterplot
ggplot(data, aes(x = ID, y =
Name)) + geom_point()
```

10. Statistical Analysis:
    - R offers extensive functions for statistical analysis, hypothesis testing, linear modeling, and more. For example:

```r
# Calculate mean and standard
deviation
mean_value <- mean(data$ID)
```

```r
sd_value <- sd(data$ID)
```

11. Advanced Topics:
   - As you become more proficient in R, you can explore advanced topics such as data mining, machine learning, and specialized statistical techniques.
12. Documentation and Resources:
   - Refer to R's official documentation (https://www.r-project.org/documentation.html) and community resources like Stack Overflow and R-bloggers for learning and troubleshooting.
13. Integrated Development Environments (IDEs):
   - Consider using R-friendly IDEs like RStudio, which provides a comfortable environment for coding, debugging, and visualizing data.
14. Practice and Projects:
   - The best way to learn R is by working on real projects. Analyze datasets, solve problems, and practice coding regularly to improve your R skills.

R is a powerful and versatile language for data analysis and statistical computing. It is widely used in fields such as data science, statistics, finance, and research. Whether you're working with small datasets or big data, R provides the tools and packages needed to extract insights and make data-driven decisions.

Scripting and automation languages are used to write scripts or programs that automate tasks and perform various operations on a computer or within a software environment. These languages are designed to be easy to read, write, and execute, making them well-suited for tasks that require repetitive actions or interactions with computer systems. Here's everything you need to know about scripting and automation languages:

Key Concepts:

Scripting Language:

- A scripting language is a programming language that is

interpreted rather than compiled. This means that scripts are executed line by line, without the need for a separate compilation step.

- Scripting languages are often used for automating tasks, interacting with files and data, and controlling software applications.

Automation Language:

- Automation languages are a subset of scripting languages that focus specifically on automating tasks, processes, and workflows.
- These languages are used for creating scripts and programs that can perform repetitive tasks automatically, such as data processing, system maintenance, and more.

Characteristics of Scripting and Automation Languages:

Readability: These languages are designed to be human-readable and have clear, concise syntax. This makes it easy to write and maintain scripts.
Interpreted: Scripts written in these languages are typically interpreted rather than compiled, allowing for rapid development and execution.
Platform Independence: Many scripting and automation languages are platform-independent, meaning scripts can run on different operating systems without modification.
Extensible: These languages often support extensions through libraries or modules, allowing developers to add functionality as needed.
Integration: Automation languages can easily integrate with other software components, enabling interactions with external systems, databases, and APIs.
Error Handling: They provide mechanisms for handling errors and

exceptions, allowing scripts to gracefully handle unexpected situations.

Common Scripting and Automation Languages:

Python:

- Python is one of the most popular scripting and automation languages. It has a vast ecosystem of libraries and modules for various tasks, making it versatile and widely used.

Bash (Unix Shell):

- Bash is a scripting language used primarily for automating tasks in Unix and Linux environments. It's ideal for system administration and scripting on these platforms.

PowerShell:

- PowerShell is a scripting language and automation framework developed by

Microsoft for managing Windows environments. It's widely used for system administration and automation on Windows systems.

JavaScript (Node.js):

- JavaScript, especially when used with Node.js, can be used for both front-end web development and server-side scripting, making it versatile for automating web-related tasks.

Ruby:

- Ruby is a general-purpose scripting language known for its simplicity and productivity. It's often used for automation and web development tasks.

Perl:

- Perl is a powerful scripting language known for its text processing capabilities. It's used in system administration, web development, and data manipulation.

These languages have already been taught under the previous programming languages.

Use Cases:

System Administration: Automate system maintenance, backup, and configuration tasks using scripting languages like Bash, PowerShell, or Python.

Web Scraping: Write scripts to extract data from websites for analysis, reporting, or integration with other applications.

Data Manipulation: Use scripting languages to process and transform data, such as cleaning and restructuring datasets.

Task Automation: Create scripts to automate repetitive tasks, such as file processing, report generation, and data synchronization.

Software Deployment: Automate the installation, configuration, and deployment of software applications and updates.

API Integration: Write scripts to interact with external APIs, retrieve data, and automate data exchange between systems.

Testing and Quality Assurance: Automation languages are commonly used for creating test scripts to validate software functionality.

Best Practices:

Documentation: Document your scripts to make them understandable and maintainable by others.

Error Handling: Implement robust error handling to handle unexpected situations gracefully.

Testing: Test your scripts thoroughly before deploying them in production to ensure they perform as expected.

Security: Be cautious about security when writing scripts, especially when dealing with sensitive data or system operations.

Version Control: Use version control systems (e.g., Git) to track changes in your scripts and collaborate with others.

Optimization: Optimize your scripts for efficiency, especially for long-running or resource-intensive tasks.

Scripting and automation languages play a crucial role in simplifying and streamlining tasks in various domains, from system administration to data analysis and web development. Learning these languages can significantly enhance your ability to automate repetitive tasks and improve overall productivity.